"This is the voice of a preacher with a passion, born from his roots in the grit of urban Detroit, and an imagination saturated by the visions of John the Seer on Patmos. York Moore belongs to a long line of evangelists who announce the good news of Jesus as deeply as the individual soul, and as widely as God's purpose for the healing of all creation."

Leighton Ford, president, Leighton Ford Ministries, Charlotte, N.C.

"In York Moore's book *Making All Things New: God's Dream for Global Justice,* followers of Jesus are challenged to live out the biblical mandate of walking humbly, loving mercy and doing justly. God's greatest desire is for his people to partner with him in ministry—sharing his good news, restoring creation and cultivating shalom. It is imperative that we answer his call. In this foundational work, York Moore explores what that can and should look like in the life of someone who loves God. We are reminded that although it is Christ who will ultimately set things right, we are invited and challenged to begin the renewing work today."

Kevin Palau, president, Luis Palau Association

"In *Making All Things New,* York Moore uses vivid imagery, engaging stories and biblical truth that challenge us to embrace the grandiosity of God's dream to end suffering and create a world where everyone and everything flourishes. This book will inspire, challenge and give you hope to be a socially, culturally and globally relevant Christian. I highly recommend it for anyone who wants to dream again!"

Rev. Dr. Brenda Salter McNeil, president, Salter McNeil & Associates, LLC, and associate professor of reconciliation studies, Seattle Pacific University

"York Moore has written a book that will cause you to think differently about the end times. *Making All Things New* eliminates all the sensational speculation about eschatological events and focuses on the central meaning of biblical end times teachings—the mission of God."

Alec Hill, president, InterVarsity Christian Fellowship/USA

"The God of the Bible reveals himself both as the God of justification and of justice. In this book, York Moore beautifully describes how God sovereignly and graciously demonstrates his concern for the eternal and the temporal. Sometimes evangelicals have been guilty of emphasizing one without the other, but in this book the two are beautifully brought together in a fitting articulation of Christ's lordship over the here and now and the eternal."

Lindsay Brown, international director, Lausanne Movement for World Evangelization

"Full of vision and urgency and grounded in today's challenging realities, *Making All Things New* dreams of something bigger for all of us! Moore brilliantly unveils God's global mission throughout Scripture and then compels us to join in."

Tom Lin, vice president, director of missions & Urbana, InterVarsity Christian Fellowship/USA

"York Moore is a storyteller and a dreamer. Here he engages with both God's story and God's dream to restore all of creation. But it's not a story about the sweet by-and-by, but rather about what it means for us to begin to live God's dreams today through our involvement with the work of justice around the world. The writing is winsome, the theology is thoroughly biblical, and the invitation is breathtaking. I love this book."

Dr. Stephen A. Hayner, president, Columbia Theological Seminary

"When Jesus' disciples asked him to teach them to pray, he said to pray, 'May your Kingdom come soon. May your will be done on earth, as it is in heaven' (Matthew 6:10 NLT). York Moore does us a favor by bringing us back to the important fact that Jesus came to make everything new. He came to inaugurate God's kingdom—here on earth. This prayer was not just about our arrival in heaven. York challenges us to see that Jesus called us to change both worlds: we change both heaven and earth through our partnering work with God in his mission."

Bob Creson, president/CEO, Wycliffe Bible Translators USA

"A powerful awakening to God's holiness, justice and strength. Moore offers a biblical eschatology strong enough to unite and empower the church to oppose evil and to advance the kingdom on earth as in heaven. This may scare hell out of us, and heaven into us for the world God loves. A great achievement."

Kelly Monroe Kullberg, author, *Finding God Beyond Harvard: The Quest for Veritas*

MAKING
ALL
THINGS
NEW

God's
Dream
for
Global
Justice

R. YORK MOORE

IVP Books

An imprint of InterVarsity Press
Downers Grove, Illinois

InterVarsity Press
P.O. Box 1400, Downers Grove, IL 60515-1426
World Wide Web: www.ivpress.com
E-mail: email@ivpress.com

InterVarsity Press® is the book-publishing division of InterVarsity Christian Fellowship/USA®, a movement of students and faculty active on campus at hundreds of universities, colleges and schools of nursing in the United States of America, and a member movement of the International Fellowship of Evangelical Students. For information about local and regional activities, write Public Relations Dept., InterVarsity Christian Fellowship/USA, 6400 Schroeder Rd., P.O. Box 7895, Madison, WI 53707-7895, or visit the IVCF website at <www.intervarsity.org>.

All Scripture quotations, unless otherwise indicated, are taken from the Holy Bible, New International Version®. NIV®. Copyright ©1973, 1978, 1984 by International Bible Society. Used by permission of Zondervan Publishing House. All rights reserved.

While all stories in this book are true, some names and identifying information in this book have been changed to protect the privacy of the individuals involved.

Cover design: Cindy Kiple
Images: © Claudia Dewald/iStockphoto
Interior design: Beth Hagenberg

ISBN 978-0-8308-3779-3

Printed in the United States of America ∞

Library of Congress Cataloging-in-Publication Data has been requested.

P	18	17	16	15	14	13	12	11	10	9	8	7	6	5	4	3	2	1
Y	27	26	25	24	23	22	21	20	19	18	17	16	15	14	13	12		

Contents

1

Dreams of
Another World

• • •

I don't usually wake up laughing, but that morning I did.

Head pressed deeply into the dense pillow, I awoke to my own laughter. The room was cold, which had caused me to sleep more deeply than usual. My legs were numb, but I was warm all over, except for my nose. A single beam of dusty light revealed an unfamiliar room of placard signs, mass-produced art and sterile chairs. Hotel room curtains never fully close, do they? A strip between the two panels allowed that beam of light to poke me in my sleepy head. I had slept so deeply that my first thought in that refrigerated state was, *Who am I, and how did I get here?*

I wanted to disappear under the thick comforter, to roll my head between the three pillows and just dream. But I had laughed myself awake. I have no idea what I dreamt of that caused such morning hilarity, but as I flopped over, sitting next to me—also laughing—was my new bride. We had been married just three days.

"What were you dreaming of?" she asked, snickering. "I watched you toss and giggle for ten minutes before you woke up."

"I wish I could remember," I said with a laugh. Though the details of the dream were lost, I knew I had tasted another world. The dream had trailed off as light hit my head, and it was gone. Nothing left now but bad breath, a lined face and a deep sense of rest and peace. Though the dream had vanished, I lay there in the bed on my honeymoon with contentment and joy.

I wish I could have held that moment forever. It was a moment between two dreams—one an unconscious dream of peace and joy, and the other a waking dream of marriage with my new wife, Jodi, where everything was new and exciting.

THE REALITY OF DREAMS

Waking or sleeping, dreams play a significant role in being human. As we slip away into the night or doze off poolside on a vacation, our hearts and minds wander to a place just around the corner, a world we've all tasted but can never quite capture. This sense of another world is, for many, a more constant, more present reality than what we are told is "the real world."

What is it about a dream that beckons us, ever entangling us in its web of hope and longing? The elusive dream of our hearts fades out of reach each morning. With each sunrise, with each knock on the door, we awake with a realization that real life awaits us. But we long to go back, to pull the covers over our faces, to tuck our heads between the pillows and just dream.

Though the elusive dream of our hearts fades, we search for it because we've tasted it in small doses over and over again. In the breathtaking beauty of a sunset, the oblivious, innocent laughter of a child, through forgiveness and kindness, in expressions of love and selflessness, we've tasted a world we were meant for and want more of. Our soul remembers the aftertaste of a world we were destined for, because we have tasted it in small measure our whole lives. The taste is unmistakable. We know this taste of the world more viscerally than anything else, because it is at the core of what it means to be human. The dream is a foretaste of another world, a better world, a world where things are the way they're supposed to be.

We are dreamers, every one of us. John Lennon's song "Imagine" described a dream where the world would one day live as one. The dream Lennon sang of—though many would disagree with him—is a reflection of this other world, a world where greed, possessions, hunger, violence, nationalistic and religious beliefs no longer drown out love, companionship and peace. Lennon's dream was very close to the dream of God, though Lennon himself would likely dismiss this. The amazing thing about the dreams of some of the people furthest from God is that their desire for a better world mirrors the ultimate dream of God to make all things new. We are dreamers because God is a dreamer.

Some have had their dreams crushed; others have been conditioned to curb or abandon their dreams. Still others, at the end of a long process of hurt and pain, find themselves no longer able to dream at all. But we all start out dreaming. We all long and reach and hope and pray and plan for something else. We are God's daughters and sons, and as such we bear the image of our creator. What we know for sure is that he is a dreamer, because at the very core of our being, we are too. Dreaming is an inescapable part of what it means to be created in God's image.

Though we are often not able to articulate it fully, what we dream of is the same dream that God has dreamt since time began. The dream of God is at the heart of our dreams. We can know a great deal about our dreaming God by looking at our own dreams and the dreams of humanity throughout the world.

Dreams are powerful, but because the world is not the way it's supposed to be, our dreams are often twisted—mere shadows of what they once were. Dreams can become misguided—expressions of exploitative power, excessive material acquisition, sensual indulgence. There's no limit to how badly dreams can run amuck. Dreams can become nightmares, ruling and eventually ruining our lives. The longing to escape the struggles and disappointments of this world often tempt us to escape "reality" artificially. Drugs, alcohol, shopping, sex, pornography—anything to escape and "just be." To be alone with ourselves, at peace with our mind, free from worry and pain— we just want to dream.

The longing to be transported from where we are to where we were meant to be is also powerful. Most people will risk everything they have and all that they are to reach for a dream. Some people do this in ways that are healthy and life giving, but most people settle for the easy substitute. We settle for a cheap version of the dream in a one-night stand, in dancing erotic pixels in dark rooms. We want a quick fix, and we find it at the baked-goods section at the grocery store, the bottom of a bottle or the pulsating floor of a dance club. We often pursue a dream in selfish and destructive ways, ways that are incompatible with God's dream.

We long to go to that other world that lingers in our hearts. We are called to it in small ways each day. For me, it is the small "magical moments" of life that call me back, the little things that pull at my heart: a wispy meadow in late August, the sound of cicadas buzzing in the trees, the smell of dense, warm air before a storm. All of a sudden, my mind wanders away from my son's orthodontics bill, the fight I'm having with my wife, Jodi, or the diaper that needs to be changed. Another world pokes in as I smell bacon in the morning or catch a glimpse of a hummingbird hovering over the lilies outside my office window. We live in a world where "real" is limited to what we can see, hear, smell, touch and taste. But these are hints of a world more real than what all our senses can tell us. Our dreams point us to another world.

WAKING FROM THE NIGHTMARE

This book explores the reality of this other world. We will also look at the nightmare that our world has become and what God has done and will do to bring an end to that nightmare. It's my contention that God began to put an end to the source of the nightmare of our world through the work of Jesus on the cross and through his resurrection. But Jesus' death and his return to life are not the end of the story. We will see that God's dream will be realized by a second, equally significant work of Christ at the end of time. Much of this book will focus on this second, end-time work.

Unfortunately, eschatology (the study of last things) and prophecy have become somewhat of a carnival sideshow over the last century. This cottage industry of future-casters and late-night preachers has made the study of end-time prophecy an almost shameful aspect of Christianity. However, the end-time work of Christ is the fuel for Christian mission, the joy in our suffering and the hope for the church around the world. It is the very culmination of the dream of God, the beam of light invading this world's nightmare. It is the most significant event in history, because within it we see the purpose of the cross and the resurrection ultimately fulfilled.

We see the nightmare of our world in the oppression of the weak and marginalized, in the exploitation of natural resources, in crippling diseases and poverty. It lives in brothels where young girls are a commodity, in the brick kilns where children waste away and in the lost hope of child soldiers. The world we live in is caught between two worlds—a dream and a nightmare.

But the good news is that the dream of God will come to pass and is coming to pass all around us. It will one day replace the nightmare of this world. In many ways, God's dream is already breaking in. Every time a well is dug for a community, food is provided for the hungry, nets protect those at risk of mosquito-borne malaria or those who traffic in the flesh of prostitutes are brought to justice, the nightmare ends and the dream begins.

When we join God in bringing his dream to the world around us, we are fulfilling his plan and purpose for our lives. Joining in God's dream is the most significant thing we could ever do. It is what we were created for. God's plan for us begins and flourishes as we allow our dreams to merge into the great dream of God.

Lying laughing and cold between two dreams that morning, I had no idea what a picture God had given me of his ultimate plan for my life and for the world. God's ultimate dream is a dream of love and laughter, of companionship and peace. It is a dream for all peoples to experience what I had in that moment of dusty light—love, joy and peace.

God's dream, and the dream at the core of our being, goes beyond justice, beyond sustenance, beyond bare necessities. It is seen in lavish celebration, in exquisite beauty and in full and lasting peace. This is what we will see as we journey together into the dream of God.

2

Between Two Dreams

• • •

Ice pellets stung my face like bees as I lay face up, entangled in a bush three days before my wedding day. Stunned, I lay there staring up at a gray March sky, assessing the pain in my ankle and calling out for someone to help me. I was just leaving my in-laws' home, where we had finalized last-minute wedding plans. A severe ice storm had moved in unexpectedly, and my broken ankle and the slick streets landed me on my soon-to-be wife's couch overnight.

Through this experience, I began to get a glimpse of the cost of marriage. I watched my fiancée struggle with my injury, bringing me soup and pillows like my new mother. She particularly struggled at the wedding when I showed up in a cast—not the dream she had of her special day. The greatest challenge came on our honeymoon; she had to push me around Disney World in a wheelchair for a week and do all the driving around town. We were given a "handicapped access" hotel room and had difficulty boarding shuttle buses and getting in and out of crowded areas. We were beginning the dream of marriage with some significant and unexpected challenges.

At the end of each day, my wife and I were exhausted. Weariness turned into a lack of patience, which turned into some real fights. Fights in the early years of a marriage are different—the rules haven't been set, so we are unaware of just how deeply we can wound each other with our words. There isn't yet the long-term demonstration that neither of us will leave if things get too bad. I was beginning to realize through my own physical pain and the newfound relationship difficulties that my dream was going to come with a cost. How high a cost? I had no idea.

I was caught between two dreams. The first was that of easy companionship, of amusement park rides and bouquets, of early-morning giggles and lingering kisses. The second wasn't a dream at all—it was a nightmare. It was the nightmare of harsh words, hurt hearts and the insecurity that comes with not knowing how things will end up.

Real dreams usually cost more than we bargain for. This was true of my dream of marriage. All my life, I longed for a home of beauty, order, safety and kindness, primarily because my home growing up did not include those things. For part of my childhood, I lived on the streets of Detroit—in abandoned homes, in the back of a van, on the basement floor of a dusty church. My childhood was the casualty of a destructive relationship between my mother and father that was doomed to fail. Throughout my childhood, I often told myself, *I'm going to do better in my home. There is no way I'm going to live like this when I get married.*

Though I had wanted to marry by the time I was sixteen, I got married much later, at twenty-seven. Finally, my dream had come true; I was waking up to companionship, friendship and partnership. Marriage is not a fanciful dream in which all of our wants come true. It's hard, soul-cleansing work. But, at its best, marriage is a small actualization of a greater dream.

A DREAM OF LOVE AND COMMUNITY

What I didn't fully realize in my idealized stupor of newly wedded bliss was that the gift God had given me in my wife, while a costly gift, was a piece of heaven itself. Marriage is a picture of the overarching dream of God. It is the picture we find where the Bible begins and, as we shall see, where it ends.

When God wanted to create a being that reflected himself, he created a community, not a person. God lives in relationship with himself—Father, Son, Holy Spirit—and the being God created was a relationship, not an individual. In the opening story of the Bible, God in community created a community that reflected himself.

> Then God said, "Let *Us* make man in *Our* image, according to *Our* likeness; and let *them* rule over the fish of the sea and over the birds of the sky and over the cattle and over all the earth, and over every creeping thing that creeps on the earth. God created man in His own image, in the image of God He created him; *male and female He created them.*" (Genesis 1:26-27 NASB, emphasis added)

Three times this passage explains that God created this "being" in his image. But it's not a singular person who ends up being the possessor of God's image; instead, it's a community— Adam *and* Eve. God's creative work culminates in the word *them*.

This initial creative work gives us an indication of what God has dreamt of since the beginning of time. The original dream of God culminates in a communal world, full and well cared for. The next few verses give us a glimpse of what God's fulfilled dream looks like:

> God blessed them; and God said to them, "Be fruitful and multiply, and fill the earth, and subdue it; and rule over

the fish of the sea and over the birds of the sky and over every living thing that moves on the earth." Then God said, "Behold, I have given you every plant yielding seed that is on the surface of all the earth, and every tree which has fruit yielding seed; it shall be food for you; and to every beast of the earth and to every bird of the sky and to every thing that moves on the earth which has life, I have given every green plant for food"; and it was so. God saw all that He had made, and behold, it was very good. And there was evening and there was morning, the sixth day. (Genesis 1:28-31 NASB)

The launch of God's dream begins in a place of beauty and order, where two people in partnership with God himself begin an epic journey of filling and ruling the world. In this passage, God tells humanity to fill and "rule" or "subdue" the created order. The biblical meaning of the words *rule* and *subdue* reflects more the idea of ordering and caring for the world than using or dominating it.

All of this is significant as we consider the dream of God. Much of the history of the world is a series of false attempts to mimic the ultimate dream. God's dream is a dream of love, of mutual respect and community. God's dream reflects care and concern for others and for the created order. In the beginning, it was good. In fact, it was very good.

THE COST OF THE DREAM

After graduating from college and embarking into industry and eventually full-time ministry, I bought a home, met my wife, Jodi, and quickly pushed for our wedding date. That whirlwind period was filled with hope and a certain sense of arrogant entitlement—my own personal dream was beginning to come to pass. I had done well, very well, for myself. I had mastered school, I had mastered business, I had mastered ministry. Everything was going well, so how could I not master marriage?

I know now that marriage is not something to be mastered—it masters us! Marriage is an ongoing, up-and-down journey of intense joy and connection as well as hard work, pain and sacrifice. Jodi and I have come to realize that now. The pain of the incompatibility of my personal dream with the reality of marriage has taken me to the brink of despair, to deep depression and to some dark places in my soul. But over fifteen years of marriage, the process of the journey has changed me in such a foundational way as to make me more fit for marriage, and for heaven as well.

So it is with the dream of God. God's dream is much more like the picture of pain and joy, sacrifice and satisfaction than the all-too common view of comfortable mansions, forever sunsets and golden harps. The dream of God comes with a high cost—a cost few anticipate.

We live between two dreams. One is a dream of a world to come—one of companionship, safety, peace, joy and love. The other is a nightmare of despair, fear, want and uncertainty. The world we now live in is not the dream of God. In fact, it is far from it. The reality is that we are not yet fit for the dream of God. We only *become* fit for God's dream through a painful adjustment process, much like the one I've been going through with my wife for the past fifteen years of marriage.

We all know that we were made for something more, something magical. But we are often confused and disappointed because the world we experience is nothing like what we were meant for. We can't experience it without what I call a "translation." The translation of our souls comes as we enter the process of becoming fit for the dream and not at home with the nightmare of our world. This process of translation does something beautiful and radical within us. It gradually tears us away from our attachment to this world, making us fit for the world to come. This painful process unfolds in different ways and at a different pace for each of us, but we must go through it.

Our dreams and the dreams of humanity throughout history have often been incompatible with the dream of God. Our dreams are often born out of greed, lust, selfishness and fear. But God is good and merciful. Most importantly, God has a plan to make all things new, and it begins when we choose to embrace the journey of transformation.

HUMANITY'S MISGUIDED DREAM

Our world is filled with real, systemic evil and wickedness—expressions of brokenness that are beyond understanding, beyond simple error or wrongdoing. This evil and wickedness is not merely around us—it is *inside* of us. It makes us unfit for the dream of God. We are not merely victims in a world gone bad; we are contributors to the wreckage of our world, and we are conduits of evil and suffering. Our personal dreams are often nothing more than expressions of this internal evil, the broken expressions of desires gone wrong. Our dreams are often destructive and doomed to fail, leaving people, the earth, communities and our own lives in ruins. To be made fit for the unfolding dream of God, we need to be translated, transformed into something more, something beautiful and whole.

At the end of time, there will come a cosmic collision between these two dreams—the dream of humanity and the dream of God. In the end, however, it is not merely us, not merely individuals, who need to be translated. *Everything* needs to be swallowed up to make room for a world that is incompatible with the one we've inherited. There is no greater symbol of the incompatibility of our world than that of the power structures and systems that comprise our cities. Every world system, every human philosophy, every exploitative economic structure has found its expression in the cities we have built for ourselves.

From the city of Babel to the final city of all time, Babylon, the grand expressions of humanity have been of exploitation, greed, lust, selfishness and fear. We read of the first great city of humankind's making:

> Now the whole earth used the same language and the same words. It came about as they journeyed east, that they found a plain in the land of Shinar and settled there. They said to one another, "Come, let us make bricks and burn them thoroughly." And they used brick for stone, and they used tar for mortar. They said, "Come, let us build for ourselves a city, and a tower whose top will reach into heaven, and let us make for ourselves a name, otherwise we will be scattered abroad over the face of the whole earth." The LORD came down to see the city and the tower which the sons of men had built. (Genesis 11:1-5 NASB)

Several striking observations help us get a glimpse into this dream of humanity. First, in this passage we see that humanity is well organized, ambitious and hard working. The builders make a plan to erect a city and a tower that is structurally sound. These goals are purposeful and attainable.

Second, their plans have a higher purpose: to unite humanity under a single name. The creativity, purposefulness, rationality and coordination all demonstrate the godlike nature of humanity—but with some big differences. Underneath this building project, we see motives of self-exaltation and arrogant self-reliance. The people say, "Come, let *us* build for *ourselves* a city, and a tower whose top will *reach into heaven,* and let *us* make for *ourselves a name*." The motive to build is born out of fear: "otherwise we will be scattered abroad over the face of the whole earth." These same motives underlie most of our cities today. This fearful reaction is inconsistent with God's dream for us to fill and order the world. Humanity at Babel, in its arrogance and self-reliance, longed to congregate, to huddle in a city of self-aggrandizement in open defiance of God's presence and plan.

This is what we see throughout time, in every city and every expression of human-centered dreaming. And it's entirely incompatible with the dream of God. In Genesis, we see God's response to our dream:

> The LORD said, "Behold, they are one people, and they all have the same language. And this is what they began to do, and now nothing which they purpose to do will be impossible for them. Come, let Us go down and there confuse their language, so that they will not understand one another's speech." So the LORD scattered them abroad from there over the face of the whole earth; and they stopped building the city. Therefore its name was called Babel, because there the LORD confused the language of the whole earth; and from there the LORD scattered them abroad over the face of the whole earth. (Genesis 11:6-9 NASB)

God observes that the power and arrogance that have come from being one people with one language can lead to a limitless expression of arrogant self-reliance and self-worship, as he says, "nothing which they purpose to do will be impossible for them." This doesn't mean that with unity we will be able to solve all our problems. Rather, with homogeneity and a godless self-reliance, there is no limit to the defiance humanity is capable of. God's dream was for the world to be filled, to be ordered, to be well managed and cared for. God's dream was for *unity in diversity,* not the eradication of differences under the banner of a human-made city built out of fear and power. God confuses the languages and separates the people, not because God dislikes unity and peace, but because in this expression of self-reliant and protective nation building, we see the seed of all evil—self-worship.

God's instructions to humanity were simple: go, be fruitful, fill and order the world. Humanity's response has quite simply been "No."

THE HEART OF EVIL: SELF-WORSHIP

Self-worship is at the heart of all kinds of evils. Greed, lust, selfishness, fear—all are forms of self-worship. The universal presence of self-worship makes us unfit for the dream of God, so we must undergo a translation process. This is a non-negotiable for participating in the ultimate purpose and goal of God. Self-worship must be eradicated in us through a painful journey, and it must eventually be eradicated from the world. And as we shall see, God will do just that.

Babel represents the core of the cosmic battle of all time, a battle of wills and desires, and ultimately a battle of dreams. This battle is not a figurative one or one that simply exists in our hearts—it is real and involves real people, real structures and real cities.

Our dream is a dream in which we don't have to trust and follow God. God's dream is a dream of expanding fruitfulness, abundance, joy and beauty. This sets us up for a conflict that must be resolved. This has happened repeatedly throughout time. The evidence of the nightmare of humanity is all around us. In every exploitative system, in every act of victimization and injustice, and in every act of indulgence at the expense of others' well-being, we see self-worship.

In Phnom Penh, a twelve-year-old girl has been sold to a brothel by her father. As a victim of her father's self-worship, she has been reduced to a solution for a desire or need that he has. She is the sacrifice to his self-worship. Every time she is raped for pay, the man raping her uses her to gratify his perverted sexual desires in an act of self-worship. The brothel owners who commoditize her flesh are worshiping self as they daily exchange her pain for their profit.

While this is most vivid in the red-light districts of Cambodia, the reality is that self-worship is at the heart of nearly every decision and every system or city that we make today. That same self-worship is at the heart of our decisions to go to porn sites and pay for the flesh of the downtrodden and oppressed, our decisions to purchase products manufactured by known violators of child labor laws, and our decisions to consume foods and beverages that come from people who receive little or nothing for their labor.

In the end, we are all Phnom Penh. We are all a part of the nightmare, and we are all unfit for the dream of God.

GOD'S COMMITMENT TO US

Yet God is good and merciful. Most importantly, God has a plan to eradicate evil and to change us, making us fit for the dream. While our dream is a never-ending string of Babels, God is at work to make all things new. So he invites us into a painful process of translation to make us fit for the dream. Though we lie face up in pain and brokenness, focused on our own selfish desires, hurling hurtful words at others and God himself, God remains committed to us and to bringing all of us into his ultimate dream.

This is why the road to the dream of God as well as the destination is depicted as a marriage. Marriage is the picture of God's commitment to us and to his dream. Throughout the Bible, those who choose to follow our dreaming God are called the "bride of Christ." How fitting! When we commit to the Dreamer, we enter a marriage relationship with Jesus Christ. We are co-owners in his great dream for us, for others and for the world.

In fact, all of divine history revolves around this aspect of God's dream—particularly that one day we will be given in marriage to Christ and will live out eternity with our partner. But before we get to that wedding day, we need to have a better understanding of the groom and the cost of making the dream a reality.

3

Power in the Blood

• • •

Our car slid on sloshy streets and in and out of the deep ice ruts that Sunday morning. The sun was fresh, hitting the slosh, making steam rise all around us like a fog machine in a movie. We left early from the abandoned building we were living in, just a shell of a home with no heat, no running water and "borrowed" electricity from an extension cord plugged into the building next door. Those days we always left early and came back late to avoid the embarrassment and ridicule from the "legitimate" poor who managed to live in the run-down houses around us.

We were on our way to something called "church," something I had never heard of in all my ten years, because my atheist parents meticulously hid all signs of God and religion. We had hit bottom, however, and this thing called church had recently provided financial assistance, food and clothes, and it was working to get us off the streets. So my mom said, "We're going to church."

Our rickety car careened off the ice and bumped into the curb as we piled out. What a sight we must have been to all those White people! We ran right up to the front door with all our wild hair, buckled shoes with no socks and obvious lack of Sunday etiquette. I wanted to see this thing called church.

At first, it seemed to be nothing more than a small building with a fat man in a hat at the door. Not what I had hoped for at all. When we walked up to the door, the fat man shook my hand and pressed me inside, saying, "Good morning, young fella." I stood feeling small in the center of the aisle at the back of the sanctuary as time seemed to stand still. The scene inside this little building was as mystical to me as the foggy snow outside. About sixty or so people stood side by side, singing, but it was like no kind of singing I'd ever heard. The music that came from my mom's AM radio carried the sounds of the Jackson 5, Simon and Garfunkel, Diana Ross and my favorite, Otis Redding's "Sittin' on the Dock of the Bay." That song in particular used to carry me away to another place. The song these strange people sang had a twang to it, but it had that same mystical pull Redding's song had. It carried the echo of a place far away, that other world I often dreamt of.

We slid into the back pew as I observed this strange world. There were lots of things I didn't understand that morning. I didn't understand what the guy up front was talking about—something about Jesus coming back and judgment. That morning, I didn't understand why people were throwing good money into that little bucket. I wished we could have scooped some out as it passed us by. I sure didn't understand why, later that morning, I was kicked out of Sunday school for something they called blasphemy.

Despite the alien nature of this encounter with church, I would remember that day for years to come. I would often sit and try to replay that song they sang, but I could never quite get it—just a broken melody and something about being free from a burden of sin.

Only years later, after I met Jesus Christ as a college student, would I fully realize what a church was and why White Southern Baptists would help Black kids with no socks and wild hair. Only years later would I rediscover the song those kind people sang with a twang: "Would you be whiter, much whiter than snow? There's pow'r in the blood, pow'r in the blood! Sin-stains are lost in its life-giving flow. There's wonderful pow'r in the blood."

These words of another world sung with confidence amid the smell of old wooden pews were the first I heard of sin and evil and blood, of cleansing and freedom and victory. Though I would not become a follower of Jesus until many years later, this strange song stayed with me throughout my spiritual journey. Because of my family's struggles with drugs, alcohol and poverty, I understood early that any Jesus worth following at all needed to be a Jesus that could save me both from the hell I was in and from the hell to come.

TOO SMALL A DREAM

Though those Southern Baptists sang about being "white" to Black kids from the streets, in practice, the Christianity they introduced me to was a faith of power, not just of another world but of action in this one. Working to help us out of poverty, those Baptists showed me both the temporal or earthly power of Christ's blood while pointing me to a message of eternal salvation.

Years after this first brush with old-timey religion, I discovered the person of Christ at the age of twenty. Unfortunately, as I began to follow this Jesus as an ex-atheist philosophy student at the University of Michigan, the Christian message I kept hearing applied this "power in the blood" only to personal sin and salvation, and not to the brokenness and suffering of the world.

I've often wondered why most Christians seem to think of Christ's work only as a work of spiritual salvation and not of world-changing power. After years of consideration, I believe I understand clearly now. I believe it is because we have relegated the good news of Christ's work merely to our own personal salvation from hell and have failed to realize the role Christ's sacrifice plays in fulfilling the global dream of God. I also believe that many of us think we can avoid the real pain of the journey of translation by making Jesus into our little pocket buddy, a good-luck charm we pull out to provide easy comfort to life's challenges.

There is no substitute for the journey, and we are either on the journey or we are not. The good news of Christ's powerful blood is that it is indeed able to save us both from the hell we are in and the hell to come—not only to save our souls, but also to transform the world around us. The basic problem of modern Christianity is that we think too small about God's wonderworking power and know little of the grandiosity of God's dream.

When we think of a homeless Black boy in the inner-city of Detroit, an eight-year-old AIDS orphan in sub-Saharan Africa or a fourteen-year-old sex slave in the brothels of Iraq, we have to realize that we don't have the luxury of choosing an either-or Jesus. The suffering and injustice of our broken world demands a solution more significant than what popular Christianity often promises; it demands a solution of power and transformation.

Amid the foggy snow of the disenfranchisement of poverty, amid the sloshy streets of the chaos of a life of fatherlessness, we are introduced to the wonderworking power of Christ's blood, which is a power of the past *and* present (and of the future, as we shall see). Jesus Christ's sacrificial work on the cross stands both within as well as above time, covering all that came before, all that confronts us now and all that will be in the end. Our world is broken, lost and in need of God's wonderworking power.

WHAT GOD SAVES US FROM

The good news of the gospel is that God desires to save us from death and hell *and* save the world from suffering and exploitation. These desires are not mutually exclusive. In his sovereignty, God does not have to choose and, indeed, he *has not* chosen between these two great needs. If we listen, we hear in the defeated whimpers of children who cry themselves to sleep hungry or cower beneath the red lights and dirty sheets of brothels that all will be healed through the wonderworking power of Christ. How can a good God ignore such realities? As we shall see, he cannot and through Christ he has not.

We need to reject the knickknack Jesus that hangs on dusty walls of dead churches throughout the world today—the Jesus who has nothing to say about the suffering of the children of the world. The Jesus we serve is able to save that boy or that girl not only from the hell to come, but also from the hell that is now. God is good, God is merciful, and God has a plan to make all things new.

Ever since coming to Christ, I've tried to understand why religious people want a Jesus who deals with the afterlife but not with the world of systems, evil power and brokenness we experience every day. Many mistakenly believe that God's divine mission revolves only around rescuing people from hell and judgment while having little to do with transforming us or the world around us. God is in the process, through the wonderworking power of Christ's blood, of making all things flourish, recreating the world. One day that work will be complete *because* of that wonderworking power.

This powerful realization reshapes what it means to follow Christ, to think of ourselves as Christians. If it is true that Christ's blood is a wonderworking power that transforms not only soul but also society, it changes the way we think of ourselves and the mission of the church. No longer is a "sinner's prayer" an insurance policy taken out against the inevitable doom that looms over the human horizon. Our commitment to follow Christ is a commitment to follow him into the world. It is a commitment to bring light into darkness and to bring real and dynamic transformation. This realization changes everything. No longer can we consider the earth as irrelevant because it is "just going to burn anyway" in the end. No longer are governments and academic institutions and economic systems irrelevant to the mission of the church.

In fact, if the blood of Christ is God's dream-making solution for the world, such enduring structures become as important to the church as the needs of the souls that compose them. This is fundamentally true because such enduring systems in their totality are what the Bible refers to as "the kingdom of this world." The dream of God is at war with the kingdom of this world, and God's intention is to subjugate that kingdom to himself through the wonderworking power of the blood of Jesus. God's dream is to make all things new.

GOD'S REIGN

At the end of time, as the dream of God begins to dawn, we see God's passion to possess the entire world.

> The seventh angel sounded his trumpet, and there were loud voices in heaven, which said: "The kingdom of the world has become the kingdom of our Lord and of his Messiah, and he will reign for ever and ever." And the twenty-four elders, who were seated on their thrones before God, fell on their faces and worshiped God, saying: "We give thanks to you, Lord God Almighty, the One who is and who was, because you have taken your great power

and have begun to reign. The nations were angry, and your wrath has come. The time has come for judging the dead, and for rewarding your servants the prophets and your people who revere your name, both great and small—and for destroying those who destroy the earth." Then God's temple in heaven was opened, and within his temple was seen the ark of his covenant. And there came flashes of lightning, rumblings, peals of thunder, an earthquake and a severe hailstorm. (Revelation 11:15-19)

In this scene, heaven stands open to earth as glory and splendor begin to eclipse the streets full of rotting refuse, the smog-covered cities and the polluted rivers. It is the beginning of one time and the end of another. One world begins to cover the other as God unleashes his great dream on the earth through his holy judgment. As we shall see throughout our consideration of the Revelation of John, through judgment, God finally asserts his lordship over all—not just over individuals but over the kingdoms of this world. Through thunder and lighting, hail and earthquake, God shakes the heavens and the earth as his final rule is announced over everything that's antithetical to his dream. In this fantastical pronouncement of his reign, all heaven erupts into worship as the judgment finally breaks upon the earth and upon those who "destroy the earth."

In this chorus of praise, we see that God's acquisition of the kingdom of the world is the cause for celebration. In the final judgment, we see the dream of God coming to pass. Praise is given to God *because* he has finally taken his great power and has *begun* to reign. This means that God has not yet taken his full power; he has not exerted his full authority in our world. He is good and merciful and has a plan to make all things new, but for now he waits for us to yield to him and avoid destruction.

This passage declares a point in the future when the waiting will be over, when God will finally begin to rule.

The dream of God is about actualizing his reign and rule over the structures and powers of this world. This is where it gets exciting for us. In our world today, we get a glimpse into this end-time dream every time God's rule is established in our lives and in our world. When a well is dug in an impoverished village, a medical clinic is built in a remote hillside community or a food distribution network is established for a famine-ravished region, we see heaven standing open.

In these moments of invading light, we see heaven exerting its rule over the chaos and injustice of our world. This is the good news of the kingdom of God. The work of the church is a work of wonderworking power, one able to transform both soul and society. The light of God's reign is breaking into our world all around us, and as it does, it prefigures the final, ultimate reign of God—when all things have been made new. In the end, not one place will remain as it is, not one place will remains untouched by the dream of God. We read this description of its totality:

> And I saw heaven opened, and behold, a white horse, and He who sat on it is called Faithful and True, and in right-eousness He judges and wages war. His eyes are a flame of fire, and on His head are many diadems; and He has a name written on Him which no one knows except Himself. He is clothed with a robe dipped in blood, and His name is called The Word of God. And the armies which are in heaven, clothed in fine linen, white and clean, were following Him on white horses. From His mouth comes a sharp sword, so that with it He may strike down the nations, and He will rule them with a rod of iron; and He treads the wine press of the fierce wrath of

God, the Almighty. And on His robe and on His thigh He has a name written, "KING OF KINGS AND LORD OF LORDS." (Revelation 19:11-16 NASB)

Again, John sees heaven standing open, and each time we see those words in Scripture, we get a glimpse into what it looks like for heaven to eclipse earth and the nightmare of our world to be overshadowed by God's dream. In this eclipse, we see a war-waging Jesus with eyes aflame with fire. In this eclipse, the Word of God comes to us not as a helpless baby, a suffering servant or a slumped-over corpse on a cross, but as the commander of vast armies, the wielder of sword and rod, a king over all kings, bringing radical and sweeping judgment against everyone and everything that's antithetical to the dream of God.

What does this mean? At the very least, it means that the dream comes with justice and holiness. The dream comes to us and our world with passion and fire. Too often, the "power in the blood" message of the church is only of forgiveness and cleansing and not of justice and radical reformation.

The dream of God can be lived out today only as we begin to understand what God is after. In the process of making all things new, God is not after our hearts alone but the whole thing—every person, every land, every system. He doesn't intend to stop until "the kingdom of this world" becomes his kingdom, until his dream overshadows our nightmare. Through Christ's sacrifice, he secured the final acquisition of all things, the purchasing of the souls of people, the triumph over all angelic powers and the subjugation of all earthly structures.

Standing between two worlds in the threshold of that Baptist church as a boy, I was introduced to a message of power and victory both for the present and for the future. With the chill of poverty and despair shrouded in foggy snow to my back, I looked onto a bizarre world of wooden pews, rituals and songs that spoke of God's great dream to make all things new. The song they sang with a twang was a melody I knew in my heart, because it came from the world I had often dreamt of. That world was one where evil was conquered and I was set free from my burdens. The wonderworking power of Christ's blood does so much more than merely save our souls from hell. It transforms the world we live in. "Would you be free from the burden of sin? There's pow'r in the blood, pow'r in the blood; Would you o'er evil a victory win? There's wonderful pow'r in the blood!"

4

The End-Time Work
of Christ

• • •

The meaning of the words of Otis Redding's song "Sittin' on the Dock of the Bay" were lost to me during my tumultuous years of homelessness and hunger as a child. Yet the haunting whistle and otherworldly lyrics of a place two thousand miles away always made me dream of another place. He sang of Frisco Bay, but to me it might as well have been in a galaxy far, far away. I had never seen a dock or a ship, though I was fond of reading of such things. This song allowed me to dream of a place where concrete didn't stretch out for miles, where time stood still and where water lapped peacefully—a place far away from the pain and want I knew in Detroit. I now know that "Sittin' on the Dock of the Bay" is a song of defeat and despair, one of arrogant escapism, but it transported me to another place every time it blared from my mom's car radio.

In the world that exists in the melody of a song that transports us away from suffering and chaos, we sense something familiar and yet just beyond our reach. It is mesmerizing.

Watch a group become entranced by a campfire. Watch as people drift off while listening to water ripple on a hot summer day at a lake. Watch as the swirling snow of a blizzard creates a holy moment for the irreverent. In all these, you will see the many ways in which deep calls to deep. Deep down, we are all connected to another place. A wide-open sky, rippling fields of grain, a rising sun, fire, water, wind, swirling clouds—all of these are commonplace elements of this world but at the same time beckon us to another place.

I fully expect to get to heaven one day, and I believe that when I get there, the greatest shock will not be how alien it is, but rather how familiar. Trees, rivers, streets, musical instruments, dancing, eating, singing—the next world is more like the one we know than we might think. Yet there is an essential difference: it is the world we know as it was meant to be. No more convoluted motives, no more hungry eyes, no more suffering and exploitation; in the dream of God, we see the world as it was meant to be.

CHRIST'S ONCE AND FUTURE WORK

This world to come is made possible because of the work that Christ has done on the cross, by the blood that was spilled to make a way for us and our world to be cleansed, to make us fit for the dream. From beginning to end, the message of our faith is a message of blood. From the sacrificial death of the animal from which God made Adam and Eve the first clothes of skin, sacrifice and blood have been at the center of God's relationship with humanity. Throughout the history of Israel, the blood of rams and bulls and lambs allowed the people of God to approach him, to be temporarily covered. When Christ appeared, John the Baptist announced to the world, "Behold, the Lamb of God who takes away the sin of the world!" (John 1:29 NASB).

The message of blood culminates in the person of Jesus, who was sent to be our sacrifice, the means by which God's dream can come to pass. Because of this, his death on the cross has a unique place in all divine history.

This message of a bloody savior has been seen rightly as the center of all divine history. After all, Jesus is "the Lamb that was slain from the creation of the world" (Revelation 13:8). I would also argue that Christ's blood figures prominently in the future dream of God, not merely in God's work in the past. This central work of Christ on the cross points to another work just as significant as his death and resurrection. The second work is the end-time work of judgment. In this work, we are introduced to the great depth of the wonderworking power of Christ's blood.

In the doorway of that Baptist church, I heard the words that have echoed throughout eternity. While I didn't recognize its melody and didn't know the words, my soul connected in that moment with the message of all time: in Christ's wonderworking blood, we have the very key to the dream of God.

The amazing reality of the work of Christ through his shed blood is that it is not merely a work of the past but also of the future. His shed blood figures prominently into the world to come, the one that lives in our hearts. In fact, God's dream can't come to pass without Christ's sacrifice on the cross. This is because Christ was the recipient of God's full, unrestrained wrath, which makes him the only one fit to enact the end-time work of judgment—it is uniquely Christ's work. It is the fact that Christ died—was slaughtered like a lamb on our behalf— that enables him to finally bring about God's global dream for all. It is this wonderworking blood of Christ that plays a central role in the end-time work of judgment.

CHRIST'S WORK OF JUDGMENT

Judgment as a work of Christ is a difficult concept for many, particularly in Western societies. Judgment has always been a normative part of God's behavior and is an important aspect of how the dream of God will be realized. Many are tempted to think that the work of judgment is only how God used to work in the unwieldy world of the Old Testament, but the reality is that because of God's holiness, judgment has been, is and will continue to be as much a function of God's core being as the many expressions of his love. God's judgment is the only way the dream of God can fully come to pass in such a broken and evil world.

In the book of Revelation, John wrote of witnessing a historic scene in heaven. In this scene, we see the divine timeline of history fulfilled. We see for the first time God taking the reins of his full authority and beginning to rule. In this historic moment, judgment is about to fall on humanity, but there is no one in heaven or earth who is worthy to bring such a final judgment.

> Then I saw in the right hand of him who sat on the throne a scroll with writing on both sides and sealed with seven seals. And I saw a mighty angel proclaiming in a loud voice, "Who is worthy to break the seals and open the scroll?" But no one in heaven or on earth or under the earth could open the scroll or even look inside it. I wept and wept because no one was found who was worthy to open the scroll or look inside. (Revelation 5:1-4)

John wept because no one was found worthy. Why?

Worthiness is a concept we don't think about much anymore, but it is central to the dream of God. In the original Greek, the word *axios* is translated *worthy*. Biblically, this concept of worthiness can be understood as either one's suitability for a task, or one's authority to comparably represent someone else in an official capacity. The word can also refer to a person's right to receive praise, dues or a reward. In Jesus Christ, because of his death on the cross, all three of these biblical meanings are applicable. Let's take a closer look:

> He came and took the scroll from the right hand of him who sat on the throne. And when he had taken it, the four living creatures and the twenty-four elders fell down before the Lamb. Each one had a harp and they were holding golden bowls full of incense, which are the prayers of the saints. And they sang a new song: "You are worthy to take the scroll and to open its seals, because you were slain, and with your blood you purchased men for God from every tribe and language and people and nation. You have made them to be a kingdom and priests to serve our God, and they will reign on the earth."
>
> Then I looked and heard the voice of many angels, numbering thousands upon thousands, and ten thousand times ten thousand. They encircled the throne and the living creatures and the elders. In a loud voice they sang: "*Worthy is the Lamb, who was slain,* to receive power and wealth and wisdom and strength and honor and glory and praise!"
>
> Then I heard every creature in heaven and on earth and under the earth and on the sea, and all that is in them, singing: "To him who sits on the throne and to the Lamb be praise and honor and glory and power, for ever and ever!" The four living creatures said, "Amen," and the elders fell down and worshiped. (Revelation 5:7-14, emphasis added)

First, in this passage we see that this "Lamb" is found to be the only one "worthy" (suitable to take the scroll of judgment) precisely *because he was slain*. Christ's suitability to judge comes from the fact that he *has* been judged. Just as the full, unrestrained wrath of God was poured out on him on the cross, so now we shall see the unrestrained wrath of God poured out on the world. God poured out all his wrath "into" his Son on the cross. As the possessor of the full wrath of God, Jesus will dispense this wrath on the world. Jesus is a "suitable" judge precisely because he was slain.

Second, Jesus represents God in his great judgment because he is seen as one with God, receiving the exact same praise, placed in the exact same position of adoration and celebrated in the exact same manner as he who sits on the throne. Jesus is praised for purchasing people from all nations and languages, from all ethnic groups and all national allegiances, and for this he is ascribed wealth, power, wisdom, strength, honor, glory and praise by the entire host of heaven. Just as the one who sits on the throne is worshiped, so is the Lamb who was slain.

Third, Jesus is seen as worthy and deserving of praise, dues and rewards *because of* his actions to purchase humanity for God and put those purchased on the pathway to purpose, toward the dream of God. The passage of praise culminates with *every* creature in *every world* ascribing praise to "him who sits on the throne and to the Lamb." Both receive the same worship and are ascribed the same worthiness. Jesus is the *comparable* judge because he is one with him who sits on the throne. Jesus is the *suitable* judge because he himself was the recipient of the full, unrestrained wrath of God. Jesus is the *rightful* judge because he has received the full recognition as the sole purchaser of the nations, the redeemer of all, through his work on the cross.

CHRIST'S WORK OF FLOURISHING

The dream of God requires justice that the rightful judgment of God alone can establish. The good news of the Christian message begins with the battle that was won on the cross through the death of Christ. This first work of Christ makes way for his second, end-time work—judgment.

What practical difference does this make in our lives today? After all, isn't the gospel the simple message that Christ died for sins, was raised on the third day and is Lord of all? In a word, yes, but the implications of this good news for the end-time work have long been absent in our understanding and missional practice.

Let's explore one practical implication. Christians have put far too much emphasis on being saved *from* and not enough on being saved *to*. Christ saves us from something (sin, death, hell and disease, poverty, exploitation), but more importantly, he saves us to something as well—to live with purpose, to make an impact in the world, to experience his love, to give him praise. Ultimately he saves us to flourish.

It's a both/and view of salvation. God's dream from the beginning was never merely a dream to restore what was lost or broken but also to cause all things to flourish, to make all things new. This is the goal of all divine mission—to make all things new and, in so doing, to cause all things to flourish.

God's holy actions of wrath and destruction are just as necessary as God's love, mercy and forgiveness for making all things flourish to his glory. As we explore the visage of a war-waging God in the next chapter, we'll see how central these actions are to the being of God and his overarching dream for the world.

Within this blessed book of Revelation, we see God's wonderworking power in action. While the victory was won against sin, death, hell, poverty, disease and exploitation on the cross, the actualization of God's victory isn't seen until his dream finds its fulfillment:

> Then the angel showed me the river of the water of life, as clear as crystal, flowing from the throne of God and of the Lamb down the middle of the great street of the city. On each side of the river stood the tree of life, bearing twelve crops of fruit, yielding its fruit every month. And the leaves of the tree are for the healing of the nations. No longer will there be any curse. The throne of God and of the Lamb will be in the city, and his servants will serve him. They will see his face, and his name will be on their foreheads. There will be no more night. They will not need the light of a lamp or the light of the sun, for the Lord God will give them light. And they will reign for ever and ever. (Revelation 22:1-5)

The dream of God is a dream of flourishing for everyone and everything: the intertwining of urban infrastructures with agriculture, water, food, healing and international peace. These are the contours of the dream of God that span all human and divine history. Embedded within the otherworldly words of that simple hymn I heard as a child was the truth that God's power is wonderworking; it is capable of changing time and space, continents and countries—and also of changing the lives of those who suffer in this world and who are on their way to suffering in the world to come.

5

A War-Waging Jesus

• • •

Milan sinks down into her well-worn bed, her little legs aching and head throbbing to the beat of the ubiquitous dance music droning in the forefront of the red-lit shop. It's two in the morning, and she sits mourning her lost childhood, a childhood stolen from her by over twenty men a day for the past seventeen months, two weeks, three days and now fourteen hours.

Each day the memory of their grotesque clenched faces and the groans of their anger and sexual release slither away like their cigarette smoke, rising and squeezing into the small hole above her bed and into the night sky. In the beginning, she tried to will herself to rise like smoke, to fly away with their stench into the night air. But now her legs ache, her head pounds, and all she can do is try to slip into a world of dreams, with memories of a life long lost.

She rocks herself to sleep, remembering the hours spent playing hide and seek with her older sister, the stories told by the old man at the fruit stand back home, the memory of something sweet on her ninth birthday, the last one spent in her disheveled little hut. Her home had no red lights, no damnable dance music and no cigarette smoke—just tin walls, a small table where her mother sat singing and the sounds of children playing outside. What she wouldn't give to rise like smoke and float away to another world.

Apart from our angst and anger for Milan's plight, her story reminds us of something important: suffering is real, and evil still churns in the human heart. Remembering is a part of remaining human, of retaining our sense of grandeur and frailty and our incredible capacity for real evil. For many, real evil vanished long ago in the killing fields, the concentration camps and the bursting hulls of slave ships. Only every now and then do we revisit evil in small doses—a campus shooting, an act of bigotry, a child's molestation. But the perpetrators of such evil are different, aren't they? They are alien, a throwback to a more ignorant and primal time, right? If we are honest, however, what is most disturbing is how familiar their actions are, how very near they are to what lives in our hearts as well.

In our day, evil has been romanticized, relegated to the status of myth and portrayed for us as hard-bodied, happy, teenaged vampires. But the myth is all too real as modern-day vampires prey on the flesh of young girls and boys, drinking their youth and absorbing their souls in the brothels where countless children are lost. Their grotesqueries, hidden for now, are no less the face of hell on earth than the acts of all despots that seem to rise and fall throughout every time and among every people. Our cyclical suspension of belief in evil gives rise to the cancerous growth of such wickedness. This growth in our day has spread to every continent and is victimizing the daughters and sons of every people.

The dream of God will not only end suffering; it will also usher in eternal justice through God's judgment. This judgment is an important work of grace in the world, for in the final judgment, we see the end of the tyranny of the nightmare for Milan and for countless others.

WHEN GOD POURS OUT WRATH ON INJUSTICE

In the book of Revelation, we see Jesus Christ, the worthy lamb, break the seals of the great scroll of God's judgment. This judgment culminates in a final, unrestrained act of pouring out the wrath of God (Revelation 16). A loud voice from God's temple tells seven angels to "go and pour out on the earth the seven bowls of the wrath of God" (Revelation 16:1 NASB). The number seven is significant in the Bible; it represents completion, perfection and totality. In what is about to come, as God poured out his unrestrained wrath on Christ on the cross, our war-waging Jesus is about to pour back this same unrestrained wrath on the world—to prepare the earth for unleashing God's dream.

In the subsequent verses, we read of horrific sores; seas, rivers and springs turned to blood; the sun scorching the nations; great darkness; and water drying up before a startling announcement. In verses 16:17-20, we have one of the most significant pronouncements from God since time began:

> Then the seventh angel poured out his bowl upon the air, and a loud voice came out of the temple from the throne, saying, "It is done." And there were flashes of lightning and sounds and peals of thunder; and there was a great earthquake, such as there had not been since man came to be upon the earth, so great an earthquake was it, and so mighty. The great city was split into three parts, and the cities of the nations fell. Babylon the great was remembered before God, to give her the cup of the wine of His fierce wrath. And every island fled away, and the mountains were not found. (NASB)

The loud voice from the temple cries, "It is done." These three little words are some of the most significant in all Scripture, for they represent the end of God's grace to the world and the final pronouncement of judgment. In fact, all divine mission points to this day of days when God finishes his missional work and finally begins to take up the reigns of his power.

"It is done" appears in a significant moment in divine history. This phrase ties Christ's work on the cross with his work of end-time judgment. In an eschatological sense, it ties the first Christ-event of the cross to the end-time Christ-event of judgment in the following ways.

First, before Jesus went to the cross to take the wrath of God onto himself, he instituted the celebration of communion in Matthew 26: "Then he took the cup, gave thanks and offered it to them, saying, 'Drink from it, all of you. This is my blood of the covenant, which is poured out for many for the forgiveness of sins'" (vv. 27-28). The cup for Jesus symbolizes the wrath of God that he drank on our behalf on the cross. On the cross, Christ literally drank our sin.

Second, Jesus stopped to pray in the garden on the night before he went to the cross, and we read these word: "And He went a little beyond them, and fell on His face and prayed, saying, "My Father, if it is possible, let this cup pass from Me; yet not as I will, but as You will" (Matthew 26:39 NASB). For Christ, it is a cup of the unrestrained wrath of God that was poured out on him on the cross. Now, in understanding the work of Christ in his first coming, we must understand it in light of the wrath of God—the full and unrestrained fury of God's anger at sin.

As Christ went to the cross, he understood that he would be taking on that wrath intended for the entire corpus of sins throughout time and space. Trembling, sweating full drops of

blood from his brow, he went willingly to that place of grotes-
query where he was mutilated and humiliated. At the pinnacle
of this first Christ-event, we read these words:

> Knowing that everything had now been finished, and so
> that Scripture would be fulfilled, Jesus said, "I am thirsty."
> A jar of wine vinegar was there, so they soaked a sponge
> in it, put the sponge on a stalk of the hyssop plant, and
> lifted it to Jesus' lips. When he had received the drink,
> Jesus said, "It is finished." With that, he bowed his head
> and gave up his spirit. (John 19:28-30)

Jesus drank from this jar of wine vinegar symbolically representing the wrath of God. The Christ-event on the cross had its
apex as he received the drink and said, "It is finished."

Between this "It is finished." and God's announcement in
Revelation "It is done" (21:6), we see Jesus is the Lamb of God,
the full possessor of the unrestrained wrath of God. He carries
our burdens, he carries our sorrows, and he carries our sin, but
one day he will carry them no longer. He has drunk from the
cup of God's wrath, and at the end of time, he will pour back
out on the world the full and unrestrained wrath of God. Between these two pronouncements, we have an era of grace and
the good news of God's forgiveness—as Christ bears the full
and unrestrained wrath of God until it passes from him to the
world in the final act of judgment.

As Jesus Christ, the worthy lamb, begins to release the unrestrained wrath of God on the world, we read of the radical
impact this has on the earth: "And every island fled away, and
the mountains could not be found" (Revelation 16:20). This reconfiguring of the earth plays prominently in what is about to
be fulfilled as the dream of God unfolds. For the dream to come
to pass, God's judgment falls in its totality on humanity and on

the earth with such force that it literally reshapes what the earth looks like—thunder, lightning, hail; blood, sores, scorching sun; earthquakes, land mass redistribution, a blackening of the sun. God's judgment is shifting from Christ to the earth, and in this we see the dream of God being unleashed.

This is not how we like to think or speak of God. Most of the time we as Christians try to hide this portrayal of a war-waging Jesus from the world. After all, this God of wrath and violence is far less suitable to the easy, consumerist faith that allows women to be sold like products and children to die for a lack of medicine that the wealthy can purchase at any corner store. Yet this war-waging Jesus is no less real than the friend of sinners who went to the cross to bear the wrath of God on our behalf. God's wrath being released on the earth means that God's dream is being established.

If we would hear the defeated whimpers of girls like Milan, our theoretical musings on God's commitment to cosmic justice may be altered. Her aching legs and pounding head turn the questions of our day upside down. "How can a loving God send people to hell?" is replaced with the question "How can a loving God fail to provide justice against those who are complicit in such a rape of humanity?"

Many Christians today are challenging or abandoning the great, dreadful eschatological realities of hell and judgment. But a Christ without the severity of God's wrath as seen on the cross is nothing more than another modern-day, domesticated god. Such gods provide merely another happily-ever-after story that plays well to our Western myth making, where young ladies become princesses instead of five-dollar whores. Milan's stained sheets points us back to our universal plight—evil in our hearts—and the cosmic reckoning on the human horizon.

JUSTICE REQUIRES JUDGMENT

The centrality of judgment and justice in the Christian story is unavoidable, and both concepts are inextricably bound. We can't have justice without judgment.

This relationship between justice and judgment is seen in the cross as God pours out his great wrath on his Son, but this one historical act of God is not an isolated expression of his commitment to cosmic justice. The dream of God—the sum of all his aspirations and actions throughout time—culminates with the great ingathering of the nations and the wedding feast of the Lamb, where all things will be restored, and death and mourning will done away with (Revelation 21; Isaiah 25:6-8). We will examine this in the next few chapters.

Prior to this great event, however, evil will be judged and justice established. As the pronouncement in Revelation 16 is given, God now wages war on the earth through Jesus. We get a glimpse of this war-waging Jesus:

> I saw heaven standing open and there before me was a white horse, whose rider is called Faithful and True. *With justice he judges and wages war.* His eyes are like blazing fire, and on his head are many crowns. He has a name written on him that no one knows but he himself. He is dressed in a robe dipped in blood, and his name is the Word of God. The armies of heaven were following him, riding on white horses and dressed in fine linen, white and clean. Coming out of his mouth is a sharp sword with which to strike down the nations. "He will rule them with an iron scepter." He treads the winepress of the fury of the wrath of God Almighty. On his robe and on his thigh he has this name written: KING OF KINGS AND LORD OF LORDS. (Revelation 19:11-16, emphasis added)

Again, John sees heaven standing open—God's dream uncontained and now invading the nightmare of earth. This portrayal of the reigning Christ is no less Christ as the Son of God weeping in the garden or over the grave of Lazarus. It is no less Jesus as the One who healed the bleeding woman and the begging leper. "With justice he judges" gives us just as much a picture of Christ as his acts of mercy and forgiveness throughout the Gospels.

GOD AT WAR

Not only is it a true perception, but we also need a war-waging Christ to make sense of God's revelation and promises. Such a Christ helps us understand the ultimate intentions of God throughout time. God is at war. His eyes are ablaze with fire over the red lights that accentuate Milan's prepubescent silhouette. His sharp sword will strike down all empires where injustices are allowed to flourish. In this, the entire world lies under the certain wrath of God. He alone is King of kings, and he will reign only after judging the world and establishing justice for all. Without this understanding of God, the Christian message is not only incomplete, it is impotent.

God's war is not a symbolic war. It is not a mere metaphor for his hatred of sin. People often say, "Love the sinner, hate the sin," but in the great judgment of the nations, sin and sinner are one object just as Christ on the cross was the actualized object of all of God's great wrath and fury. Such things should make us tremble. Either Christ stands as our substitute, taking on the full wrath and fury of a holy God at war, or we will stand before him as the objects of his justice and judgment.

"He treads the winepress of the fury of the wrath of God Almighty" (Revelation 19:15). In wine making, grapes are corralled in a container, smashed to a pulp and then pressed. This is not total obliteration or annihilation but destruction so severe and complete that it transforms the object being crushed into an indistinguishable mass, forever incapable of being restored to its prior form. In this, we see God's reconfiguring work on humanity and on the physical earth as all mountains and islands flee from his presence. The phrase "the fury of the wrath of God Almighty" points to the manner with which the act of crushing will be done. For now, God's fury remains hidden, contained in the person of Christ, but the full, unrestrained expression of God's rage is just beyond the horizon. Such a historic moment should strike real fear in the heart of every person.

Milan's plight is not out of the sight of the all-seeing God. Her defeated whimpers fuel the great wrath of God against the nations. The promise of Scripture is not merely that our sins can be forgiven or that Milan's tears will one day be wiped away, but also that her captors will be crushed like grapes. They will be pressed out under the full, unrestrained wrath of God. God is at war not only _against_ injustice but also _for_ those who suffer.

We need to recapture the centrality and motivating nature of the eschaton, to recommit ourselves to the study of prophecy and redeem the hope we have in the personal return of the war-waging Christ. When the great eschatological realities of the Christian faith are ignored or allegorized, we lose the ability to provide a cohesive, comprehensive worldview. As a result, the Christian message itself is compromised. We can't have the great love of God without the great wrath of God.

In one bookend, Christ on the cross says, "It is finished." In another bookend, the loud voice from the temple pronounces, "It is done." There we see Christ unleashing the full, unrestrained wrath of God. In this wrath, we see God's actions to establish justice in the earth as well as his dream for the nations.

The cross alone can't give us God's ultimate answer for suffering and injustice. The judgment poured out on Christ on the cross is only a part of God's plan. God is at war, a war that was won in the devastating blow against sin and death on the cross, but one that will be won only when heaven stands open and the rider on the white horse comes forth with his armies to once and for all banish evil from his world.

Milan's suffering will be replaced by the joy of the great wedding feast of God. No longer a five-dollar whore, she will be free to experience this time of great joy and renewal. In this alone do we see her tears wiped away and the music and red lights of her hell vanquished forever.

6

A Global Invitation
of Joy

• • •

Joy has a possessing power over us. Real joy has a tendency to run away with our reason; it causes us to throw caution to the wind and to forget.

My fiancée and I sat giddy at a table, planning the guest list for our wedding. Joy had overtaken us as we began amassing a guest list of monstrous proportions. Jodi, my now-wife, has always had more friends and much more family than I, but I had many people to invite as well. Our list ballooned from the one hundred guests we had originally discussed to well over three hundred. As we wrote down name after name, the excitement of seeing the faces of the people who had become important to us seemed so much more important than the cost of feeding them or the available room in the church's fellowship hall.

"How can we not invite Al?" I would say, for example. Al was a one-legged, ex-con street preacher I had grown to love.

"I know, I feel the same way about my third cousin on my dad's side," she would answer. She had seen that third cousin once as a child at her grandfather's farm, but joy had come to possess us.

We had a real problem: we had to get the number of guests down to fit within our budget. Despite hours of trying to figure out who was essential to include, we made little to no progress. Eventually three hundred people attended our wedding day, and all of them ate very well. Joy found a way.

All divine history is moving toward a day of joy, a day filled with the faces of the people who will have responded to God. There's nothing God will not do to fill his wedding hall to capacity. He is inviting all of humanity to the celebration he has in store. Throughout history, God has pointed to this day of joy in nearly every book of Scripture. I don't understand how it will work, where all the people will sit or what they will be fed, but I believe joy will find a way.

A WEDDING AND THE STORY OF GOD

When Jesus launched his public ministry, he did so at a wedding. At the wedding at Cana, he not only blessed the institution of marriage but also gave us a picture of the abundant, possessing joy of the great wedding day of God. After the host of the wedding ran out of wine, at his mother's request, Jesus instructed the servants to fill six stone water jars usually used for ritual purification and then to draw water out to take to the chief servant. As they followed Jesus' instructions, the simple water was transformed miraculously into a wine that was more than sufficient—wine that was praised as the best wine of the evening (John 2:1-12).

We learn about the dream of God from this story. After the wine was served, "what Jesus did here in Cana of Galilee was the first of the signs through which he revealed his glory; and his disciples believed in him" (John 2:11). In turning water into wine, Christ performed not only the miraculous but also what

John referred to as a "sign" pointing to the ultimate intent of God in divine history. This act of turning water into wine was a token, a partial glimpse into an event to come and into the unique role Jesus will have in that event.

John recorded that Jesus "revealed his glory" in this act, which caused his disciples to believe in him (John 2:11). When Jesus wanted to reveal who he was and what he was ultimately after in the world, he didn't begin by healing someone from sickness, raising the dead, casting out demons or correcting philosophical/theological errors—all very important works. He began to reveal his glory and his unique place in history by turning water into wine at the height of the joy and excitement of a wedding feast for two anonymous people.

Throughout the Gospels, Jesus told many wedding stories— a great wedding banquet, the marriage supper of the Lamb, the marriage feast for the king's son, and the man who had no wedding garment. In his seminal work, *Announcing the Kingdom: The Story of God's Mission in the Bible,* Arthur Glasser says that the wedding feast parables "all refer in one way or other to the same apocalyptic event (Luke 14:16; Rev. 19:9; Matt. 22:2, 11). And yet the impression is given that the festive spirit of that future banquet can be enjoyed even now, as it is connected with the mission of the church."[1] Glasser sees the wedding feast motif as central to the story of Christ's mission and as connected with the eschatological event referred to as the marriage supper of the Lamb, described for us in Revelation 19 and 21.

Divine history is moving toward this event. It was foreshadowed throughout Scripture through wedding after wedding, story after story. From the introduction of Eve to Adam to the story of the love and union of Isaac and Rebekah, all the way to the wedding of this anonymous couple at Cana, God's story has been one of love symbolized in the union of husband and wife. God loves weddings because the union of the two becoming one is the very story of God.

DON'T MISS THE PARTY

At a dinner party with Jesus, a man possessed by joy shouted out, "Blessed is everyone who will eat bread in the kingdom of God!" (Luke 14:15 NASB). His response came out of exuberance after hearing Jesus' instruction that those who give banquets ought to invite the poor, the crippled, the lame and the blind because they can't repay the host, yielding a blessing of repayment at the end of time, during the resurrection of the righteous. This guest's excitement over Jesus' instruction was likely as a result of the anticipation of the resurrection in general, a hotly contested idea during Jesus' day, and not because of the inclusion of the outcasts in the story. This is seen in the details of the story Jesus told:

> But He said to him, "A certain man was giving a big dinner, and he invited many; and at the dinner hour he sent his slave to say to those who had been invited, 'Come; for everything is ready now.' But they all alike began to make excuses. The first one said to him, 'I have bought a piece of land and I need to go out and look at it; please consider me excused.' Another one said, 'I have bought five yoke of oxen, and I am going to try them out; please consider me excused.' Another one said, 'I have married a wife, and for that reason I cannot come.' And the slave came back and reported this to his master. Then the head of the household became angry and said to his slave, 'Go out at once into the streets and lanes of the city and bring in here the poor and crippled and blind and lame.' And the slave said, 'Master, what you commanded has been done, and still there is room.' And the

master said to the slave, 'Go out into the highways and along the hedges, and compel them to come in, so that my house may be filled. For I tell you, none of those men who were invited shall taste of my dinner.'" (vv. 16-24 NASB)

Jesus reiterated that the master's banquet is open to the poor, crippled, blind and lame, but we learn from this story that it is rejected by a variety of people who have become preoccupied with worldly affairs. Because of their rejection for seemingly good reasons, the joy of the host is scorned. There is great humiliation on the part of the joyful when others denigrate, disrespect or disregard their joy.

In this story, the scorning causes what seems to us to be an overreaction. The dinner host becomes angry and compels his servants to go into the streets and to invite anyone and everyone "so that my house may be filled." The dinner host's main concern is that the party be filled, that the joy and celebration that comes with a large crowd be experienced at his banquet. We sense the host's anger in his final words, "None of those men who were invited shall taste of my dinner." This anger indicates that, in the mind of the host, nothing is more important than this feast—not business transactions, not investments, not even the celebration of one's own marriage. The dinner host's party is in his mind the very center of existence.

It's astounding that Jesus included this reference to a man who wants to be excused because he has just married his wife. This seems to fly in the face of the centrality of the wedding concept, but Jesus' story leaves no room for misinterpretation. This banquet, which is too similar to other stories of the wedding feast of the Lamb to ignore, is the banquet to end all banquets. It trumps all earthly celebrations or commitments, because it is God's great banquet.

We also see the universality of the invitation—even the crippled and poor get in. Jesus told this story at what likely was a lavish and formal gathering. Street people with their obnoxious smells, wounds, lack of manners and disheveled clothing would have been incredibly offensive for those present. But God's great banquet is to be a celebration of joy, open to all people, perhaps particularly to "the least of these." In God's mind, this is the most important thing in all the world.

GOD'S GUEST LIST

This banquet feast of God was fresh on my mind as I bounced up and down in the back of a World Vision truck on a dusty road in Svy Pok, Cambodia. Svy Pok is a rural village just outside Cambodia's capital city, Phnom Penh. I had become aware of Svy Pok years before through undercover video footage revealing the rampant sex tourism there, particularly of prepubescent children.

Svy Pok is a place where children roam naked in the streets along with mangy dogs and loose cows. It is a place of steaming pots of unknown scraps, a place of diseased water and HIV/AIDS victims. It is a place where the rich come to pay to rape children, to slice away their innocence and to take advantage of a vulnerable people. The exploitation, sickness, hopelessness and poverty of Svy Pok make it one of the most unlikely places to find joy. It is one of the modern-day places Jesus referred to in this story as "the hedges," communities on the outside of infrastructure and organized resources. The people of Svy Pok are the kind of people the host compelled his servants to invite to the feast. Through the work of World Vision, they are getting God's lavish invitation and will find their way to his great celebration.

As we bounced in and out of the craterlike potholes on the streets of Svy Pok, I thought of God's great wedding feast and how the poor of Svy Pok would beat most of us to God's table.

Naked child after naked child lined the street, waving and running after our truck. *These are God's little ones*, I thought.

We pulled up to a brightly decorated structure filled with children and teenagers, smiling, laughing and well dressed. They were members of World Vision's community program for at-risk youth. After practicing their English, making warm welcomes and joking a bit, the teens of the center put on a rather long play for me on how they educate their village to fight human trafficking and the victimization of women and children in general.

After this moving display of community empowerment, we walked over a makeshift bridge and down a back alley to another World Vision complex, where their child-protection team sat waiting to educate us on the changes they've seen as a result of working directly with the village leaders. Empowering village leaders and working with community gatekeepers and local law enforcement seemed to be changing the practices of traffickers and steering would-be sex tourists away from the village.

During the presentation, a young girl the age of my daughter back home caught my eye. My wife and I had just adopted a two-year-old girl from the U.S. foster care system. Here, a world away, was another little girl who could have been my daughter's sister, except for the color of her skin and cultural distance. I watched this little girl as she giggled, as she played with a broken toy in the corner, as she ran after a chicken that managed to skirt by the open structure. Despite the very moving presentation I received from my friends at World Vision that day, the joy amid poverty and suffering I saw in her eyes said it all.

God's dream is one of joy, and his invitation is an invitation to all. The children of Svy Pok are at the top of God's invitation; they are among the ones who will fill his hall with laughter. God's guest list is ever expanding; he has no interest in whittling it down. God's wedding hall will not run out of wine, will not be short of delicacies and will not be unoccupied. God will make sure of it! Thanks to the servants of organizations like World Vision, God's invitation is going out to the highways and hedges of this world—to the poor, crippled, blind and lame—to the least of these.

PREPARED FOR THE FEAST

On my wedding day, as I looked out on my guests and the smiling faces of well-fed family, I saw a picture of the day of days, the end-time culmination of God's long-dreamt dream. My banquet was wall-to-wall full. The sound of music and laughter echoed down the halls of the church; food covered ornate tables decked out with flowers and ribbons; speeches and memories were shared; and an overarching joy filled the air. If the joy that comes with the celebration of a wedding can be experienced in this world, what of the joy that comes with the wedding of all time in the next?

After the defeat of the enemies of God at the end of time, we see the cessation of the exploitive practices of those who sell women and men as slaves and their grotesque transactions of a pay-for-rape industry. In Revelation 18, God judges the kings of the earth who commit fornication by visiting the brothels of the world and the merchant rulers who grow rich by buying and selling souls. Along with the "great city" described as Babylon (v. 16 NASB), these merchant rulers and kings are finally judged, and the response in heaven is breathtaking.

> After this I heard what sounded like the roar of a great multitude in heaven shouting: "Hallelujah! Salvation and glory and power belong to our God, for true and just are his judgments. He has condemned the great prostitute who corrupted the earth by her adulteries. He has avenged on her the blood of his servants." And again they shouted:

"Hallelujah! The smoke from her goes up for ever and ever." (Revelation 19:1-3)

Judgment, condemnation, vengeance, wrath—these are the precursors to the great announcement that God's wedding feast is ready because it is the prostitution, the adulteries, the unjust shedding of blood that stand as an affront to the invitation. God's dream can't come to pass while women, men, boys and girls lie strewn in the dusty alleys of rural villages, while prostitutes sit waiting for sex tourists, while women are ravaged by AIDS and children continue to die of malaria. Evil and human suffering in this realm must be done away with.

Unfortunately, most evil and suffering are not simple by-products of a world in free fall. Behind most suffering is a monstrous face: someone profiting from pain. Behind the defeated whimpers of children who cry themselves to sleep are the wealthy and well fed who could have done something but chose to ignore the need. Either through the remote consumption of goods and services that come at the price of human lives or through direct exploitation and victimization, most suffering in the world is our fault. In the end, however, Babylon (both real and figurative) will be destroyed.

Babylon is both a real place and a representation of every exploitative system that creates merchant kings and geopolitical tyrants. Both will be cast down with smoke that will rise forever and ever, and then the end will come.

We read these breathtaking words heaven has longed to proclaim since the Fall:

Then I heard what sounded like a great multitude, like the roar of rushing waters and like loud peals of thunder, shouting: "Hallelujah! For our Lord God Almighty reigns. Let us rejoice and be glad and give him glory! For the wedding of the Lamb has come, and his bride has made herself ready. Fine linen, bright and clean, was given her to wear." [Fine linen stands for the righteous acts of God's holy people.] Then the angel said to me, "Write this: Blessed are those who are invited to the wedding supper of the Lamb!" And he added, "These are the true words of God." (Revelation 19:6-9)

Joy. Like the roar of a mighty tidal wave—shouting for joy. After the defeat of God's enemies, God is praised because he finally reigns and his dream can come to pass. The bride has made herself ready with bright and clean, fine linens. These fine linens are the righteous acts of God's holy people, but notice that these linens are "given her" (v. 8). Our righteousness comes as a gift from God, and all righteous acts are made possible only because of the grace and empowerment of God. We will be clothed—made acceptable—to participate in this day of days because the Lamb was slain, providing the righteousness necessary to gain entry into the wedding feast of all time. This is a prerequisite for being able to experience the dream of God. Without the righteousness of Christ—these clean and bright linens—we will never experience the joy of this day.

Nothing unholy, nothing unclean is acceptable in God's wedding banquet. All must be cleansed and made righteous. In another story, Jesus told of the wedding feast of God:

The kingdom of heaven is like a king who prepared a wedding banquet for his son. He sent his servants to those who had been invited to the banquet to tell them to come, but they refused to come. Then he sent some more servants and said, "Tell those who have been invited that I have prepared my dinner: My oxen and fattened cattle have been butchered, and everything is ready. Come to the wedding banquet." But they paid no attention and went off—one to his field, another to his business. The rest seized his servants, mistreated them and killed them. The king was enraged. He sent his army and destroyed those murderers and burned their city. Then he said to his servants, "The wedding banquet is ready, but those I invited did not deserve to come. So go to the street corners and invite to the banquet anyone you find." So the servants went out into the streets and gathered all the people they could find, the bad as well as the good, and the wedding hall was filled with guests. But when the king came in to see the guests, he noticed a man there who was not wearing wedding clothes. He asked, "How did you get in here without wedding clothes, friend?" The man was speechless. Then the king told the attendants, "Tie him hand and foot, and throw him outside, into the darkness, where there will be weeping and gnashing of teeth." For many are invited, but few are chosen. (Matthew 22:1-14)

Matthew's version of this parable is similar to the Luke passage earlier noted, with some key exceptions. First, those who are initially invited refuse to come, they pay no attention and in the end actually mistreat and kill the king's servants. The fact that this host is specified as a king makes the rebellious actions of those refusing the banquet particularly distasteful. Their actions are an assault not only on the celebration of the wedding but on the very kingdom of the king. They are actions of war.

Another key difference is that the servants bring in the good as well as the bad to fill the hall. The word for "bad" in the text implies a person of moral want, an immoral person. The king notices this person not because of his actions, but rather because of his lack of proper clothing. Without the clean linens and clothes we obtain through the righteousness of Christ, we are unfit for God's wedding feast.

Notice also that condemnation and punishment await the man, who is bound hand and foot and thrown into a place of darkness and suffering. Why? Without the righteousness that comes from Christ, we are all partakers in Babylon, complicit with those who destroy the earth and exploit the poor. We are as those who pay to rape children or profit from the products made off the backs of slaves. We are either made clean and bright through the righteousness of Christ, fit for the dream of God, or we are bound hand and foot and cast out into the darkness. There is no middle ground.

God's happily ever after is a day of celebration with a banquet hall full and pristine. It is a day of joy and celebration. In this vision of God's wedding feast, we see the ultimate fulfillment of a familiar celebration. It is the culmination of all history, the ingathering of all peoples from the highways and hedges of this world. It is a lavish celebration for the poor, the blind and the lame—all made acceptable because of the finished work of the Lamb.

7

The Wedding
of All Time

•••

Dust clogged my nostrils as I swayed back and forth in the rear of a Cambodian tuk-tuk, a motorized carriage used as a taxi. I'm sure that Phnom Penh will become one of our world's great cities someday, but for now it is a mixture of extreme poverty and towering new buildings. Dirty tuk-tuks battle on the hot, dusty streets alongside Land Rovers and Lexus sedans. Most streets in Phnom Penh are hardly wide enough for the traffic that crams together from every direction.

Day after day, on my journey back and forth throughout this bustling city, I was amazed to find entire blocks closed with large, ornate tents sitting in the *middle* of the streets. They were wedding tents, so it didn't take long for me to realize how important weddings are in the Cambodian culture. One of the great aspirations of young girls in Cambodia is to become a cake maker for these weddings or a dressmaker for the brides. There are entire industries devoted to providing tents and wedding décor for these street festivals—all in celebration of the union of the small or great, rich or poor.

What surprised me most, however, was not the lavish nature of these enormous celebrations but how little their presence seemed to bother the angry and aggressive drivers battling to traverse the narrow streets. I asked my driver about this, and his response said it all: "In Cambodia, there is almost nothing as important as the wedding day. It is very, very important. Tent weddings happen all the time. It is just a part of who we are."

God's culture parallels in many ways the people of Cambodia. For the Cambodian people, the wedding celebration is a part of who they are. In their wedding culture, they have unknowingly placed the aspirations of the living God at the very center of their streets and their national story. In a dirty place of hostility and want, the Cambodian people are happily inconvenienced by beauty and hope.

I believe the Cambodian tents of marriage are a clue as to why the wedding motif is so important to God's great story. To understand God is to see the centrality of the wedding celebration—it is the culmination of his great dream! For those of us who would be followers of the dreaming God, we must understand that lavish celebration, overwhelming joy and deep communion are a part of God's "culture." Like the Cambodians, God is not inconvenienced by the celebration of love or the intrusion of joy.

The lavish way in which many embark on the marriage journey as portrayed is a small picture of the dream of God. Before the creation of the world, before time began, God dreamed of a great day of union between him and his people. This dream of God is so great that nothing will deter it from coming to pass—not the fall of his creation, not the willful determination of the devil, not the death of his Son Jesus and not the rage of the nations. God will have his day.

God officiated the first wedding when he presented Eve to Adam in Genesis 2. Jesus' first public miracle was at the wedding in Cana. The author of Hebrews tells us that marriage is to be held in high honor as a sacred institution. Paul spoke about marriage, saying, "This mystery is great; but I am speaking with reference to Christ and the church" (Ephesians 5:32 NASB). The Bible tells us that the union of husband and wife is a picture of a greater union between God himself and his bride, the church. One day, the Bible tells us, God will make his dwelling with his bride. One day we will be reunited with God at the wedding feast, the fulfillment of the eternal dream of God.

The great eschatological wedding feast of God is spoken of so clearly in both the first and second testaments that it is hardly possible to understand the Bible's story without it.

We get a breathtaking look of this future day in several places in Scripture.

A MOUNTAIN OF CELEBRATION

In the book of Revelation, we have a fantastic account of dragons and beasts, disasters and death, astronomical anomalies and celestial courtroom drama. But for all its imagery and foretelling, Revelation is mostly about God's wedding invitation to the world. At its height, John's vision explicates the greatest wedding of all time—an amazing event of restoration, redemption and rejoicing. Revelation is unique not only in its genre type but also because within it we hear the trumpets sound and see God himself descend on the wedding of all time.

The Revelation of John is the only book in all Scripture that comes with a promise like this: "Blessed is he who reads and those who hear the words of the prophecy, and heed the things which are written in it; for the time is near" (1:3 NASB). It is also the only book in all Scripture that comes with a warning like this:

I testify to everyone who hears the words of the prophecy of this book: if anyone adds to them, God will add to him the plagues which are written in this book; and if anyone takes away from the words of the book of this prophecy, God will take away his part from the tree of life and from the holy city, which are written in this book. (Revelation 22:18-19 NASB)

Why such promise? Why such warning? Because to God it is the most important day in all history! This is the story of God's wedding, the culmination of his dream since before time began: what was lost in the garden, was restored in the resurrection and is now realized at the wedding feast on the mountain of God. In Revelation 21 we are introduced to the venue for the dream of God, a mountain of celebration for all the nations to enjoy.

Those who have planned a wedding day know that the place itself is important— so important that people spend thousands of dollars decorating and accessorizing it. For the wedding of all time, God has chosen a lush and transcendent mountain.

Then one of the seven angels who had the seven bowls full of the seven last plagues came and spoke with me, saying, "Come here, I will show you the bride, the wife of the Lamb. And he carried me away in the Spirit to a great and high mountain, and showed me the holy city, Jerusalem, coming down out of heaven from God." (Revelation 21:9-10 NASB)

In every instance where the Scriptures tell us of God's wedding day, the setting is a mountain of celebration. Scripture says that it will be *the only* mountain. God will demolish all mountains: "Every island fled away and the mountains could not be found" (Revelation 16:20). We don't know if this refers to the specific region where John sees this vision or if it is global (I favor the former), but the reality is that there will be a radical reconfiguration. When judgment finally comes to the earth, God will remake the very surface of the earth. He will exalt his holy mountain and distinguish it from the rest of the terrain. While we can't be sure what the final renovation of the entire world will look like, we know it will be dramatic.

GOD'S PREPARATIONS FOR THE FEAST

In Isaiah, we read further about the radical nature of God's work of restructuring the world:

> Behold, the LORD lays the earth waste, devastates it, distorts its surface and scatters its inhabitants. And the people will be like the priest, the servant like his master, the maid like her mistress, the buyer like the seller, the lender like the borrower, the creditor like the debtor. The earth will be completely laid waste and completely despoiled, for the LORD has spoken this word. (24:1-3 NASB)

As God prepares to act on his ultimate intention to be one with his people, he purifies the earth and prepares it for the wedding of all time. In this vision we see not only the hope and aim of all mission but also the great dread that comes from a determined God who will have his way. The wedding of the Lamb is a holy moment planned from before the foundation of the world.

We get a more detailed look into this wedding feast in Isaiah 25:6-8:

> On this mountain the LORD Almighty will prepare a feast of rich food for all peoples, a banquet of aged wine—the best of meats and the finest of wines. On this mountain he will destroy the shroud that enfolds all peoples, the sheet

that covers all nations; he will swallow up death forever. The Sovereign LORD will wipe away the tears from all faces; he will remove his people's disgrace from all the earth. The LORD has spoken.

The grand vision of God culminates with wine and feasting, with joy and deep connection with God himself for all the nations. This, in the end, is the focus of the Christian faith—it was God's desire from the beginning. It is what was lost in the garden and what God has been at work to restore ever since.

Notice that it is Yahweh (YHWH), the Almighty, who prepares the feast (v. 6). He does not coordinate the feast through some human or angelic agency. He himself prepares the feast of joy. Notice also what he prepares: rich food for all peoples, aged wine, the best meat. This celebration is so much more than mere sustenance; it is lavish in every way. It is extravagant in the identity of the host, in the venue on this high mountain and in its fare. The vision of God is a celebration, a mountaintop feast of momentous proportions.

A MOUNTAINTOP EXPERIENCE

Mountains are important to God. Throughout the Bible, God uses a mountain to stage his grand and sweeping eschatological movements. The Law was given to us on the mountain of God. The Israelites first worshiped God after the Exodus on the mountain of God. On mountains, Jesus preached, fed hungry people, prophesied the coming future kingdom and was transfigured before his disciples. On a mountain that will one day be lifted to the heavens, Christ ascended and will descend to bring about this everlasting kingdom. The mountain is a sacred place for God.

The author of Hebrews said this about the new mountain of God:

For you have not come to a mountain that can be touched and to a blazing fire, and to darkness and gloom and whirlwind, and to the blast of a trumpet and the sound of words which sound was such that those who heard begged that no further word be spoken to them. For they could not bear the command, "IF EVEN A BEAST TOUCHES THE MOUNTAIN, IT WILL BE STONED." And so terrible was the sight, that Moses said, "I AM FULL OF FEAR AND TREMBLING." But you have come to Mount Zion and to the city of the living God, the heavenly Jerusalem, and to myriads of angels, to the general assembly and church of the firstborn who are enrolled in heaven, and to God, the Judge of all, and to the spirits of the righteous made perfect, and to Jesus, the mediator of a new covenant, and to the sprinkled blood, which speaks better than the blood of Abel. (Hebrews 12:18-24 NASB)

Justice and peace are established on the mountain of God by the Judge of all through the new covenant in Christ's blood. You see, this mountain of God is where heaven meets earth, where God sits down with his people, where healing and shalom and flourishing are established.

So holy is this day on the mountain, so sacred is the wine that we will drink at this feast, Jesus made a pledge concerning it. After instituting communion for the church, he said, "Truly I say to you, I will never again drink of the fruit of the vine until that day when I drink it new in the kingdom of God" (Mark 14:25 NASB). The passage in Hebrews connects Revelation 21 and Isaiah 25 with the pledge of Jesus in Mark 14. This is the day Jesus spoke of, the day when the kingdom of heaven dawns, when suffering and injustices end. The covenant that God made with Israel on a mountain through the Law has been subsumed in the new covenant in the blood of Christ, which will culminate in the kingdom when we drink together with God at this feast.

The dream of our heart is anchored in God's dream, realized on the mountain of God. For all humanity, this day of days lives in our heart as the image bearers of God. It's the epicenter of another world we've long dreamt of. It's the world that lingers in our mind like a faint memory, a distant smell—something familiar yet alien at the same time. The kingdom of God is just out of reach for now, but we hunger for it every day. We long for God's kingdom—for beauty and order, for peace and flourishing. We long for joy.

A MISSIONAL DREAM

Revelation 21:5 tells us that God is on a mission to make everything new. The church's mission and the desire of our heart is to bring God's kingdom in its fullness to bear on our world. We long to see people come to Christ. We long to see communities restored and economic and racial injustices reversed. We long for the creation to be restored and for the world's poor and marginalized to have justice. We all know there is another world peeking through the veil, poking into our world, tearing at the fiber of this dying universe. This is what our hope is based on—another world, which dawns with the great wedding feast of God. I believe that this hope can spark the flame of revival in our lives and in the church; this anticipation of a coming kingdom can awaken Christians to the power we have right now through the resurrection to transform our society and culture. In other words, our conviction around God's coming kingdom enables us to live into that kingdom right now.

As Christians, we are called to live into this great day right now. The church is not an institution deployed by God to manage sin or to preserve culture, but rather an unstoppable force sent into the world to transform the soul as well as society. This unstoppable force is intended to make ready a people fit to partake in God's day of joy and union. The vision of the church is ultimately one of celebration and joy born out of resurrection. However, this is not a vision of some far off, distant time but of right here, right now. Our mission is to send an invitation to the world, an invitation for a magical moment on the mountain of God, an event long dreamt of by God for all, but also an invitation to live into that moment now.

Our dreams need to be much bigger. The grandiosity of God's dream requires us to reach much further than we typically do in mission. Too often we satisfy ourselves with incremental missional advances, with man-sized visions and woman-sized plans. We satisfy ourselves with stemming the tide of brokenness, pain and injustice. We think of caring for victims of forced prostitution, of providing medicine, of rescuing people from hell with the gospel and engaging godless philosophies through the art of apologetics. All of this is good, but God's dream is so much bigger, because it's rooted in this divine day of celebration. It isn't merely one of restoration, but rather of abundance and flourishing.

Divine history ends with the marriage of God's people to himself. In the wedding feast, we see the cessation of separateness, the end of loneliness, the beginning of community and of new life. God is on a mission to make all things new, and on the mountain, at the wedding feast, we see the whole, final fulfillment of his dream—and we are called to live into this dream right now. We bring the future joy of the wedding feast of God into the lives of the invited guests through Christian mission; mission is nothing less than this. Mission is ultimately the work of inviting the world to be one with God, to join in not as an observer but as the bride in the greatest wedding of all time—God's wedding!

God has always longed to be one with his people; this longing marked the very passion of Christ. Before going to his death, Jesus prayed,

> The glory which You have given Me I have given to them, that they may be one, just as We are one; I in them and You in Me, that they may be perfected in unity, so that the world may know that You sent Me, and loved them, even as You have loved Me. Father, I desire that they also, whom You have given Me, be with Me where I am, so that they may see My glory which You have given Me, for You loved Me before the foundation of the world. (John 17:22-24 NASB)

Jesus envisioned that we would be one with him just as he is one with his heavenly Father. This was his mission in coming to earth and going to the cross—to prepare a people that he could be one with. Every human wedding points us to God's great obsession, which will one day be fulfilled at the marriage supper of the Lamb.

This day of holy union comes at a great cost to God as well as to us and our world. We can't get to the tents of joy and to the table of celebration unless we deal with the obstacles to that day. Unless we deal with the dirty streets and the exploiters, this day is nothing more than a dream. But as we shall see, God does indeed have a plan to make all things new.

8

A Distant Thunder

• • •

Wooden pews rocked to the sound of electric guitars. As the crowd whipped into a frenzy, the wild-haired pastor in a flamboyant silk shirt shouted many times, "Jesus! Jesus! Jesus!" People began to cry and run around as I sat dumbfounded. This was very different from my first encounter with old-time Baptist religion just a few years before.

There were no hymns about the power of Christ's blood in the charismatic church I ventured into that day, but plenty of songs about the power of the Spirit. The whole place felt chaotic, and it made me both excited and a bit scared at the same time. When church dismissed for Sunday school classes, those in their early to mid-teens were instructed to go across the street to the barn. After following the crowd of tight pants and silk shirts, I was amazed to arrive at a literal red barn; I had thought it was a figure of speech. As a city boy, I had never been inside a real barn with actual hay and rafters.

Compared to the full-bodied older teens, I felt like a child with scrawny, scraggly wisps under my lips and unfashionable clothes. I guess I didn't get the memo that it was 1981, and silk and corduroys were "awesome!" The whole experience felt very much as if I had entered another world. And what happened next didn't fit any world I had encountered in all my twelve years either.

"You know Jesus is coming back. Who's ready for J-E-S-U-S?" the youth pastor said, looking very much like a mini-me pastor in his own tight pants and silk shirt. "I said, who is ready for J-E-S-U-S?!" he said even more fervently, but this barn crowd wasn't so excitable. The teens clustered, chatting and playing around. The youth pastor said, "Today, we are going to finish up our film on the return of Christ."

After he called for the lights, the movie, filled with more teens in tight clothes and wild shirts, explained the basics of Bible prophecy and how Jesus Christ could return at any moment. It was this "at any moment" repeated throughout the film that caught my attention. While many teens in the barn slipped outside to kiss and smoke, the urgency of the film's message riveted me.

In one scene, a young man explained to a bunch of teens that Jesus could come back at any moment and that the Holy Spirit was preventing the world from falling into chaos. He said that the evil one, the antichrist, would one day appear and force everyone to receive a mark on their hand or forehead to enable them to participate in a global economy. The teen actor went on to explain that Christ would one day return to judge the world with fire and to make war with the beast. In a seven-year period called the tribulation, people would suffer before the end of the world.

As an atheist, I had never heard of these things. It had never occurred to me that the world may have a preset "end of the story." This didn't seem to be the happily-ever-after I thought Christians believed in. My mind began to swirl, in part from the strange new assertions I was hearing and in part from the scent of marijuana flowing in through the window.

Just then, the youth pastor shut the film down and screamed at the teens just out the window, "B-I-L-L-Y! Is that you smoking weed again at my barn!" After exchanging a variety of 1980s curse words, Billy said, "Maybe I'm the antichrist!" and stuck out his tongue and hands to make an obscene gesture. He vowed never to return and stomped off with a girl on each arm, defiantly strutting, still with his marijuana cigarette dangling from his lips.

The youth pastor tried to draw the session to a close, but it was chaos. The teens all wandered off in clusters except for me. I left that strange place in a fog, stumbling back down the street to meet my mother and brothers. From the church service with tight pants to a screaming pastor and rocking pews to a barn filled with the smell of marijuana and talk of the mark of the beast, I left certain of one thing: this kind of Christianity was the most bizarre thing I had ever encountered.

I went through the next few years as an atheist but still pondered that youth group encounter from time to time. The song that played in the movie rang through my head: "I wish we'd all been ready . . . " I would often lie awake, thinking, *What if I'm wrong? I know there is no God, but if I'm wrong and J-E-S-U-S comes back, I'll be just as bad off as B-I-L-L-Y!*

Throughout my teens, I would often sneak off to look at my porn collection and my secret New Testament with Psalms and Proverbs. This little book was just as much a source of shame and mystery to me as the glossy pages of my growing pornography collection, hidden under the tacked-down carpet. I read only Revelation, searching for any confirmation of the message I had encountered in that film. I read of beasts and dragons, of angels shaking the heavens and blotting out the sun. I read of blood and hail, of sharp tongues and a lake of fire—all just as esoteric and mysterious as the posed bodies of *Playboy* and *Penthouse*, and every bit as fake to me. The world of Bible prophecy seemed too fantastical to be true, too horrible, too otherworldly.

God's otherworldly dream is a dream of flourishing, of gathering the nations and people from every beautiful language and cultural manifestation. Though it is fantastical, I believe all of it is true, from dragons and beasts to hail, blood, sharp tongues and a lake of fire.

What I didn't realize the first time I encountered these ideas portrayed in the film and the bizarre world of charismatic Christianity in the late seventies and early eighties was that Bible prophecy had gone through an intense period of commercialization and speculation in the United States. As a teenager, I was encountering an American religion that had been whipped into a frenzy by an army of tightly clothed, emotional preachers who were certain that Jesus' return was just around the corner. The problem with much of the Bible prophecy movement of the time was its emphasis on the wrong aspect of God's dream. As a result, the exciting implications of the return of Jesus were also out of place.

PROBLEMS WITH PROPHECY

Eschatology, the study of "last things," is the study of God's story—the journey God has been on since the expulsion of Adam and Eve from the garden. It is the overarching story of God's plan to bring all things together for his glory and purpose. The Bible prophecy movement in America robbed the global church of our passion for God's overarching story in three ways.

First, with all its associated prophecy superstars, conferences, books and films, the movement placed nearly all its emphasis on the return of Jesus and the rapture or the removal of Christians from the earth before the final judgment. While these components of God's story are important (Jesus will return, and God does have a plan to judge the world), that's not how the story ends. The story ends with joy and celebration; it ends with a mountaintop feast of justice and relational reestablishment. The story ends, not with the destruction of a city, but with the creation of one. Jesus' return and the judgment of the world is a dreadful and very real component of God's "end game," but it is not the hope of the Christian faith.

Second, the Bible prophecy movement of that era emphasized fear and separation from the world rather than joy and cultural engagement. Whipping people into a heated frenzy through images of the antichrist forcing people to receive the mark of the beast and of people being thrown into the lake of fire placed the emphasis on personal holiness and separation from the world. While personal holiness is important in the life of a believer, it's no more important than our mandate to go into the world, to engage it with the gospel and to make disciples of all nations.

This leads to a third excess of the Bible prophecy movement of that era. It stressed individual witness *at the expense of* social action. To some, the rationale is that if the world is going to burn along with the body of sinners, our work as Christians should be to save souls, not care for people's temporal needs, the earth or our communities. The goal, then, is individual conversion, no matter what. There's something profoundly sad and delegitimizing about this distortion of the Christian faith. While it's not heretical, it's so far from the whole story of God as to make the Christian faith seem like nothing more than an escape raft from the rising floods of suffering. It ignores God's love for the nations and his plan to restore all things. A partial story of the Bible does more harm to would-be followers of Christ and the mission of the church than our total abandonment of the Bible.

Years later, at seventeen and in a drunken stupor, I stumbled into my shack of a house at two in the morning. I grabbed some cold chili off the stove, turned on the television, whipped out my porn and Bible, and sat glued to the words of a late-night Bible preacher. While he didn't have the same wild shirt and wasn't screaming J-E-S-U-S, this slick-suited, gray-haired Bible thumper sang the same song as the film. "Don't you know that AIDS is a judgment from God on all the foul homosexuality in our land! The aborted babies in this country since Roe v. Wade scream out to us! Their blood is on our hands!"

More religious nonsense, I thought. My cold chili was just as obnoxious to me as that guy's opening lines. For a moment, Ms. January's glare caught my eye, and I drifted before the words strung from the bloated, mannequin-like preacher: "Thessalonians tells us that it will happen in a twinkling of an eye, that at *any moment* Jesus will return and that he will judge all the dirty rotten sin in our land. Friend, are you ready for J-E-S-U-S to return?"

For twenty more minutes, the preacher pulled a stream of Bible verses together that portrayed this same picture of blood, hail and fire. I could hardly keep up with the Bible references, though I managed to jot many of them down for later examination. Again, the phrase "at any moment" grabbed my heart. If I was wrong, if Billy was wrong, if the world was wrong, then at any moment we could face the music. This thought has been a part of my life ever since I encountered it in that barn.

The sense of urgency and the terrible nature of the return of Christ might have the power to scare people into temporary action, but it doesn't usually have the staying power to transform our souls, to touch our hearts in such a way as to transform us forever. Only the full dream of God can do that.

NO MORE SEA

When Christ returns, all things will be set right, justice will be restored, and the villains of the story will be judged. With his return comes God's dream of blessing for all the nations.

At the end of the story, John recorded for us several "no mores" associated with the return and rule of Christ. He wrote that he saw that there was "no longer any sea" (Revelation 21:1). I love the oceans of the world, and I've been blessed to see many of them. Oceans are a part of God's creation, full of life and mystery. When John said he saw no more sea, it doesn't mean that in the new world there will not be oceans or large bodies of water. The sea represented tumultuous chaos, nearly unconquerable barriers; for the ancients, it was where evil and death lived, and it was one of the primary resting places for the dead. Hence, before the great and final judgment, the "sea gave up the dead that were in it" (Revelation 20:13).

Also, the seas separate nations, creating distinguishable land masses or continents. This may be a consequence of the brokenness of the creation as a result of sin. I believe that at one point God's creation contained one landmass surrounded by ocean, and one day the earth may be characterized by a single landmass again. Perhaps, in this sense, John beheld a world where there is no longer any sea.

NO MORE TEMPLE

John also saw that there is no longer any temple. The temple— that special, localized place of worship—was considered to be the resting place of God, the place where one went to "see God."

But in the new world, there will be no more temple, "for the Lord God the Almighty and the Lamb are its temple" (21:22 NASB).

This truth is probably the single greatest contour of the new reality. It is the very epicenter of the dream of God, something that hasn't been true since God walked in the garden "in the cool of the day" (Genesis 3:8). This is what God is after: communion with his people, face-to-face, unmitigated relationship. John recorded this exciting reality as a voice *from the throne* announces, "Now the dwelling of God is with men, and he will live with them. They will be his people, and God himself will be with them and be their God" (Revelation 21:3).

By implication, there is *no more temple*, which means God has chosen to dwell with humanity, to live with us. The long-awaited dream of God to dwell with his creation in peace, joy and love is a result of the return of Christ.

Why wasn't this a part of the film? Why did the Bible prophecy films and screaming pastors focus only on the esoteric and bizarre and not on the wonderful and passionate love of God? Why only half the truth? What might the full story have meant to Billy? What might it have meant to me?

NO MORE SUN OR MOON, NO MORE NIGHT

In Revelation, John recorded that there is no need of the sun or moon and that there is no night there, because "the glory of God gives it light, and the Lamb is its lamp" (Revelation 21:23). This doesn't mean that there will be no more sun or moon, but rather that they are unnecessary for providing the light and rhythms of seasons and days. Our world is ruled by the cycle of day and night, seasons and time zones. We are very dependent on the role the sun and moon play—but one day, no more.

The sun and moon have an expiration date for their utility. While their beauty and grandeur may remain, the light of God, the lamp of the Lamb, will one day replace our need for sun and moon. The sun and moon were created to separate night from day, darkness from light, and to serve as the source by which time and seasons are understood and calculated (Genesis 1:14-18). But when we are face to face with the Light of lights, the source of time and space, these lesser lights have no utility. They become obsolete.

Jesus' return ushers in a time of great freedom, of liberation from the limiting resources of this world. Unending light, the cessation of night and the return and reign of Christ will bring about a lasting day and the expulsion of the rule of darkness, both figuratively and literally.

NO UNCLEAN THING

Finally, John recorded that there will be "nothing unclean" in God's dream (Revelation 21:27 NASB). Holiness is a prerequisite. The dream of God has no place for sin and brokenness, either on a personal level or on a corporate level. Those who see God's face, who are able to dream God's dream, are made clean by the righteous work of Christ. John described in at least three places toward the end of Revelation the kinds of people who are excluded from the dream of God. He wrote that "the cowardly, the unbelieving, the vile, the murderers, the sexually immoral, those who practice magic arts, the idolaters and all liars—their place will be in the fiery lake of burning sulfur. This is the second death" (Revelation 21:8).

It's interesting that cowardice and a lack of belief are in the same list as murder and sexual immorality. Courage and a believing faith are repeatedly placed at the center of the description of a person made fit for heaven, fit for the dream of God. If righteousness is portrayed as clothing, the clothes worn by those who participate in God's dream are courage and faith, not immorality, distortion or unbelief.

John noted that liars are also not fit for the dream of God. There's something terribly important to God about being clothed in truth-telling, about living honestly "without guile," as Christ observed in Nathanael (John 1:47 KJV), and as attributed to the righteous in Revelation 14:5. Dishonesty has no place in the dream of God—no masks, no fronts, no hypocrisy.

God's dream requires us to face ourselves, to face one another and to face God—to be clothed in truth. In fact, this is so important, it's the one thing that makes it on to all of Revelation's lists about those who are allowed to live the dream: "Nothing impure will ever enter it, nor will anyone who does what is shameful or deceitful, but only those whose names are written in the Lamb's book of life" (21:27). All the other characteristics of ungodliness are collapsed into the general concepts of impurity and shamefulness, but John was careful to note that the deceitful are banned from the city of God. Their names are not written in the Lamb's book of life.

John also wrote,

> Blessed are those who wash their robes, that they may have the right to the tree of life and may go through the gates into the city. Outside are the dogs, those who practice magic arts, the sexually immoral, the murderers, the idolaters and everyone who loves and practices falsehood. (Revelation 22:14-15)

Those who have "washed their robes" have the right to the tree of life and have access to the city of God. Again, the purity symbolized by the robes of white linen comes from the gift of God's grace given to us through the shed blood of Jesus Christ. Outside the gates of the city, outside of the reach of the dream of God, are a certain kind of person—those clothed in sexual immorality, murder, idolatry and falsehood.

Falsehood is so important to God that it's included in nearly every list of sins throughout the Bible. God cares about purity of personhood as much as he does the sanctity of life and sexual purity. In the dream of God, we will and must be made whole in this area. We must be rightly clothed and fit for the dream.

"Maybe I'm the antichrist," Billy had said, stomping off with a marijuana cigarette dangling and a woman on each arm. There was more honesty in his actions and admittance than meets the eye. In reality, all of us, particularly me, have stormed off from God's dream. Through lust, self-indulgence, violence, arrogance and falsehood, we are all antichrist. Sitting with my cold bowl of chili and gazing into the sultry eyes of a paper doll, I couldn't have cared less about God's dream for me or the world around me. But the fact that Jesus will return changes everything. Injustices and immorality will be judged, and the villains of the story—us included—will one day face the Judge of all time.

God's dream requires us to put away falsehood, to put on the righteousness that comes from the person of Jesus and his work on the cross and through his resurrection. Just as I stood out of place with the wrong shirt and pants, with my wispy, under-developed body in a barn of chaos and confusion that day, so without Christ we stand entirely unprepared for the great dream of God that's breaking into our world. Will we be found with clean and bright wedding linens on God's great day of feasting? Will we be rightly clothed for the return of Christ?

J-E-S-U-S is coming back, and the sad reality is that we are not ready; we live lives of falsehood, masquerading, hiding even from ourselves. The unfortunate result of the Bible prophecy movement of the seventies and eighties is that one could understand all sorts of graphs, charts and speculative timetables yet fail to have a heart of compassion and love for the nations. We can know a lot about the return of Christ and yet not be clothed, not be prepared to live the dream, to see Christ face to face.

The song in the film said, "I wish we'd all been ready," and certainly this is the cry of the Revelation of John. Preparedness is the reason Revelation is given to us—to make us ready, to warn us, to inspire us to belief, courage and obedience. John recorded these words of Jesus:

> And he said to me, "These words are faithful and true"; and the Lord, the God of the spirits of the prophets, sent His angel to show to His bond-servants the things which must soon take place. "And behold, I am coming quickly. Blessed is he who heeds the words of the prophecy of this book." (Revelation 22:6-7 NASB)

9

The End
of Our Dream

• • •

The dust cloud rushed up with my son, enveloping him as he perfectly slid into third and popped up to take the base for the winning run. It was the eleventh inning. Though the season had been an epic failure—nearly every game a loss before this one—this game was the game to end all games.

It was the last game of the season, and they were playing the most winning team in our city's Little League. Just hours before, the other team had taken the diamond in arrogance, sure to make a slaughter of the worst team in the league. But something happened early in the game—fire broke out, and my son's team took a commanding lead.

Behind me, my nine-year-old daughter ran giggling wildly with a bubble wand as smaller children chased her, enormous bubbles billowing behind her as she galloped in the green grass. My newly adopted one-year-old sat in a miniature lounge chair, cheering for her new big brother while chomping on melon as its juice ran down her sticky, brown cheeks. The sun was scorching, but a solid line of dark clouds loomed on the horizon.

As I sat watching my son, I couldn't help but stare intently at the very edge of the line of storms. The leading edge seemed to twinkle as the sun ahead struck it, making the silver edge sparkle in contrast to the blackness at the heart of the storm line. Such storms are common in Detroit and often carry damaging winds, develop suddenly and move quickly. I have learned to take such storms seriously.

The game was now in a fever pitch, and it seemed certain we would beat the almighty first-place team, a dream no one on my son's team had imagined as they suited up that afternoon.

"We can do it, guys!" my son shouted from third base. "Smash it out of the park!" With two boys on, including my son at third, all our team needed was one go-ahead run to end the game in victory.

To the plate came our best hitter, a twelve-year-old horse of a boy. He looked like a giant compared to most boys on the field. The moment seemed to stand still in time as dark clouds hung like a wall behind parents with lips pressed together, standing against the gates.

He swung and smashed a grounder through the second baseman's legs. The boys rounded the bases. As two of the three boys slid in to home plate (though they didn't need to slide), a party of dust and preteen cheers erupted as the winningest team literally burst into tears in the dugout. Just then the sky opened up, and we quickly packed away our melon-drenched baby, bubble-blowing nine-year-old and dusty son and screeched off into the blinding rain. What a day!

As we left the park that hot afternoon, we drove away from the line of storms and soon escaped the rain. Looking ahead, we could see the hot sun, kids playing in their yards and couples out on after-dinner strolls—perhaps unaware of the line of bursting thunder, lightning and rain that was just minutes behind us. Looking back, I could see the sharp, diagonal line of blackness creeping ahead, consuming the blue, ending the day of leisure for all in its path.

THE APPROACHING STORM

If ever there was a metaphor for the danger and destruction that looms on the human horizon because of the great and awful judgment of Christ, it is this stark picture of sudden transition and danger. As I gazed at the dazzling edge of the storm line, I couldn't help but imagine Jesus leading the line, bearing down on our quaint little life of melon and bubbles, dust clouds and high fives.

We live in a suspended moment, a time when it seems normal to laugh and play, to kick back and spend hours with family and friends. We live in an in-between time when the grace of God makes such moments of play and leisure possible. While there's nothing wrong with life as we know it, we need to live with the awareness that there's a dark line of storms just behind us in our rearview window, bearing down on all the world. We've lost this sense of urgency, and because of this, our lives are too focused on leisure, consumption, indulgence and play.

Living with a sense of urgency is seen as fanatical and excessive. It's mocked by talk show hosts and news anchors. But the reality is that Jesus is coming back and with him a great judgment. Day will turn to night, and reality as we know it will come to a sudden end. We can't outrun it, we can't wish it away, and we can't ignore it indefinitely. Jesus will return to judge the world, because it's necessary for God's dream to come to pass.

Many live as if the storm will never come, but the Bible assures us of its certainty. Toward the end of his ministry, Jesus

instructed his followers of the reality of this coming storm. Enamored with the beauty of the architecture of the Jewish temple,
the disciples had pointed out its grandeur to Jesus. His response
is one of the most detailed revelations of the end times in the
entire Bible. In Matthew 24, several contours of the storm are
revealed to help us understand the certainty and frightening
nature of the return of Christ.

WHAT JESUS SAYS ABOUT THE END

Matthew 24 is also known as the Olivet Discourse, because it
occurred on the Mount of Olives. Jesus taught about end-time
false messiahs, international war, famines, social upheaval, the
revelation of the antichrist and massive displacement of peoples.
In the beginning of the passage, the disciples asked Jesus three
questions that set the context for the discourse: when all this
would take place, what the sign of his coming would be and
what the sign of the end of the age would be. Christians have
wrestled with these questions for two thousand years.

Unfortunately, many have claimed more certainty than God
allows. Developing charts and graphs and sophisticated equa-
tions, well-intentioned women and men have confused many
and have left the general population anaesthetized to any talk
of the end of the world.

Jesus' instructions in the Olivet Discourse actually didn't
give the disciples the answer they sought. He didn't tell them
with any certainty when these things would happen. He didn't
give them the definitive *sign* that the end was near or that his
return was imminent. Rather, Jesus gave his disciples a glimpse
into what life would look like *as end-time events unfold.*

Most notable is Jesus' description of what it will look like as the
diagonal line of dark storms breaks on the world with his return.

Immediately after the distress of those days "the sun will be darkened, and the moon will not give its light; the stars will fall from the sky, and the heavenly bodies will be shaken." At that time the sign of the Son of Man will appear in the sky, and all the nations of the earth will mourn. They will see the Son of Man coming on the clouds of the sky, with power and great glory. (Matthew 24:29-30)

In this breathtaking glimpse into the return of Christ, we see the *sign* of the return of Jesus *in heaven*. This image of Christ returning in the sky is repeated several times throughout Scripture. Jesus said he will return "on the clouds of heaven, with power and great glory." His return will be unmistakable; it will be highly visible. It will be as recognizable as a stark line of storms against a clear, blue sky. He will return with power, not in humility, not weak and bound, but as a victorious king, judging the world. He will return with glory in a splendor and alienlike display of grandeur far outstripping any architectural grandeur humanity has ever accomplished. In essence, Jesus said to his disciples, "If you want to see glory, wait until you see me coming in the sky!"

PICTURES OF THE END

Several other passages of note reinforce our understanding of this day of power and great glory. We read Daniel's revelation of this same event:

In my vision at night I looked, and there before me was one like a son of man, coming with the clouds of heaven. He approached the Ancient of Days and was led into his presence. He was given authority, glory and sovereign power; all nations and peoples of every language worshiped him. His dominion is an everlasting dominion that will not pass away, and his kingdom is one that will never be destroyed. (Daniel 7:13-14)

In Daniel's vision, Jesus is given sovereign power over all nations and peoples, over the ethnic and cultural people groups of all the world—every language, every sector of every nation. Jesus is given an everlasting dominion that will not pass away, never to be destroyed. This is in breathtaking contrast to the perishable kingdoms of the world, like a diagonal line in the sky swallowing up all that stands before it. Daniel 7 reveals a nearly concept-for-concept narrative of the unfolding events in Revelation 13–14, where all earthly kingdoms and all demonic powers are swept away. While the events are in a slightly different order than they are recorded in Revelation, Daniel and John undoubtedly reveal the same events. Compare Matthew 24 and Daniel 7 to the opening words of John's vision:

To him who loves us and has freed us from our sins by his blood, and has made us to be a kingdom and priests to serve his God and Father—to him be glory and power for ever and ever! Amen. Look, he is coming with the clouds, and every eye will see him, even those who pierced him; and all peoples on earth will mourn because of him. So shall it be! Amen. "I am the Alpha and the Omega," says the Lord God, "who is, and who was, and who is to come, the Almighty." (Revelation 1:5-8)

John's vision provides the additional reminder that Christ loves us, that he has freed us from our sins by his blood. This is how we understand Jesus' return and the judgment he will bring with him. Jesus' sacrificial act of freeing us from sin, of paying for our debt by his blood, of making us a "kingdom of priests" to serve God—these realities help us understand the dreadful storm that looms on the human horizon.

God is merciful, and before the storm comes, he has provided a way through which we can be saved, through which we can be freed—the blood of Christ. Service, worship and freedom are all seen here as the result of Christ's first work, a work of sacrifice by which he took all the unrestrained wrath of God upon himself. As we have seen, Christ's death on the cross qualifies him to be the rightful judge, because he is currently the sole possessor of the full wrath of God. When Jesus returns, however, it will be to empty himself of this wrath, to dispense it back onto the world. These three passages detail that appearance. The return of Christ begins with a global, climactic appearance as he comes on the clouds of heaven.

TWO DESTINIES

Since the beginning, the dream of humanity has been a dream of self-reliance, of self-aggrandizement, of self-assertion. In small ways, we live entirely independent of God. We choose to work and play, to eat and drink, to relax and travel at will. We are seldom truly under the rule of Christ, living life as gods. Even the person who has chosen to live her life as a follower of Jesus generally doesn't truly live under his control except when forced to.

Only during times when we can't control our circumstances are we reminded that we are, in fact, small, like dusty children circling a baseball diamond. We can't control the real world that invades ours, the world that comes crashing in. We get a glimpse with every earthquake, tornado, flood or fire. When we feel the turbulence of a quaking airplane or feel our car skid across a sheet of ice, most of us cry out to God without hesitation.

But the reality is that the majority of our life is just as much out of our control as those moments of panic and danger. Global economic forces beyond our comprehension rock our savings, our loved ones get incurable diseases, our children grow secret addictions, our departments downsize, and our companies close. The reminders are all around us. Yet we continue chasing bubbles, covered with melon, as the seemingly endless sun beats down on our brow while disaster approaches. None of life is ours to control.

Christ's return is the greatest reminder that there are only two options: to be loved and freed by his blood or to be destroyed by his wrath and anger. Those are our choices.

Jesus said he will return on a cloud, and both Daniel and John confirm this in their vision of the future. We find more details in Revelation:

> I saw heaven standing open and there before me was a white horse, whose rider is called Faithful and True. With justice he judges and wages war. His eyes are like blazing fire, and on his head are many crowns. He has a name written on him that no one knows but he himself. He is dressed in a robe dipped in blood, and his name is the Word of God. The armies of heaven were following him, riding on white horses and dressed in fine linen, white and clean. Coming out of his mouth is a sharp sword with which to strike down the nations. "He will rule them with an iron scepter." He treads the winepress of the fury of the wrath of God Almighty. On his robe and on his thigh he has this name written: of the KING OF KINGS AND LORD OF LORDS. (19:11-16)

Jesus will come on the clouds as the rider on a white horse, Faithful and True, with justice waging war. This vision of his return should strike fear into the heart of all. All divine history is heading toward the moment Christ sweeps away the dust and lays the foundation for the very dream of God.

Jesus wages war on all demonic forces, against all geopolitical expressions of dominance, self-reliance and exploitation. Jesus destroys those who destroy the earth, who profit from the flesh of girls and boys, and who benefit from systems of poverty. These are the themes we see throughout the Revelation of John. This war-waging Jesus means business. We are either of those who are loved and freed by his blood or of those who are swept away by the sharp sword of truth that comes from his mouth.

This is a different and disturbing way to conceive of Jesus. Most prefer the baby in the manger and have been turned off to this Jesus, but only this conception enables us to make sense of the near absurdity of Jesus giving himself willingly on a Roman cross. If we understand Christ's sacrifice on our behalf *in light of* the emptying of the full and unrestrained wrath of God to come, we get a better understanding of the love and mercy of Christ.

PLEDGING ALLEGIANCE TO THE LORD

Revelation 19 refers to the armies of heaven, clothed in fine linen, clean and white. These are those who have been made pure, who have been freed and forgiven through the blood of Christ. Being freed and forgiven begins when we accept that we can't control our lives or our future. When we give up trying to be our own lords or masters, when we acknowledge the rider on the white horse as the King of kings and our Lord, only then can we join his heavenly army. The Bible tells us we become a part of Christ's kingdom, God's great dream, when we confess Jesus as Lord.

> If you declare with your mouth, "Jesus is Lord," and believe in your heart that God raised him from the dead, you will be saved. For it is with your heart that you believe and are justified, and it is with your mouth that you

profess your faith and are saved. As Scripture says, "Anyone who believes in him will never be put to shame." (Romans 10:9-11)

Becoming a part of God's dream requires us to change allegiance, to pledge ourselves to the one true Lord. Only then can we be saved. The term *saved* refers to being saved *from* the wrath and judgment that looms over the human horizon as well as being saved *into* a life of love and freedom, as we read in Revelation 1:5. When we acknowledge that Christ died to pay the penalty for our sin and rebellion, and that he is alive, risen from the dead, we also acknowledge his rightful place of leadership in our lives; we acknowledge his lordship. As Romans tells us, this is done by declaring with our mouths, by professing our faith.

As you read these words, perhaps you're realizing that you haven't yet been clothed in Christ's righteous linens, washed in the blood of the Lamb. Perhaps you have been gripped by the great love and sacrifice Christ has made on your behalf. You can be saved *from* the full, unrestrained wrath of God and saved *into* the freedom and love God has for you right now by declaring your allegiance to the one and true Lord, Jesus Christ. If you would like to be saved, you can pray aloud a prayer like this:

Jesus, have mercy on me. I believe you died for the sin of the world and paid the penalty for my rebellion. I believe you are alive, that you were raised from the dead and that you are going to return to judge the world. Make me clean, forgive me and lead my life. I accept your rule over my life.

By acknowledging these truths before God, we become a part of the people of God, the army of the dream. We are those who will never be "put to shame." When Jesus returns, the world will be shamed. The winningest team, with all its power and arrogance, will be shamed. The antichrist and all demonic forces, the powerful and oppressive world powers, those who mock and do as they please—they will all be put to shame when Jesus appears with power and great glory, riding on the clouds with justice. However, those who have placed their faith and trust in Christ will reign. They will not be put to shame but will be sheltered from the storm.

Driving out of the rain that day after my son's game and looking off into the distance at the people walking in the daylight, I was reminded just how urgent the message of Christ is. The world around us lies in the direct path of a destructive force the world has never known. Only the message of God's love and freedom can save both us and our world *from* the wrath of God as well as *into* his love and freedom.

10

Fire in the Sky

●●●

In tight, pink spandex, she struts down the block, sauntering toward the corner store, where she will sell her flesh to desperate, gritty men. Her clients pull in and out of the dirt street near the liquor store just outside my childhood home's front door. The air is cold but dense with the putrid smell of toxic waste. The blight of boarded-up homes all around and the frequent drug distribution just a block down make for a picture-perfect inner-city scene of misery and woe.

I spent most of my teenage years in this city of woe—Inkster, Michigan. Inkster is a small city just west of Detroit and is easily one of the worst parts of the Detroit area. Greater Detroit is a great place to live, and I've enjoyed raising my family here, but Inkster is a place of sorrow within a world of misery.

Inkster is easily one of the worst places I've ever been. I lived there in a shack of a home at the end of a dead-end street for over ten years. There were twenty-one homicides within a one-mile radius of my home the year I graduated high school, and police often wouldn't come when violence rang out or someone's home was broken into. Many of my friends got caught up in violent crime or drug addiction, went to prison or lost their minds during the tender years of our adolescence. The ominous "Dead End" sign in front of my home, the dense and dangerous air, and the sound of automatic gunfire each night marked this place as one of misery and woe.

Woe is a word we don't use very often, but it's one of the most significant words in the Bible. Typically, it refers to a proclamation of grief or a pronouncement of a curse or judgment. When Jesus pronounced a woe on a town or people, he always followed it up with a prophecy of doom or destruction. In Revelation, however, the word *woe* is used in a very rare noun form to refer to the comprehensive execution of plagues and disasters that compose the end-time work of Christ.[2] In Revelation, woe is no longer merely a future, predictive statement but rather becomes a time and a place where a set of cataclysmic events unfold. If God's dream is the ultimate intended state of affairs for God and his people, then woe is both the state of existence for those outside that dream and the means by which they are separated from God and his dream.

A TALE OF TWO WOES

As we've seen in Revelation, the Lamb who was slain is worthy to open the scroll of end-time judgment (Revelation 5), a scroll sealed with seven seals. The breaking of these seven seals prefigures the real judgments found within the scroll. The number seven represents completeness and finality in the Bible, so it's generally agreed that this scroll of divine wrath is sealed completely, reserved for the unrestrained wrath of God at the end of the age. The unsealing of the scroll represents the transference of the wrath from Christ to the world. Recall that this wrath was initially poured out onto Christ and held by him until the end of the age. In this transference, we see the means by which God's dream comes to pass as he eradicates all that is antithetical to that dream.

These seals are broken at last:

> When the Lamb broke the seventh seal, there was silence in heaven for about half an hour. And I saw the seven angels who stand before God, and seven trumpets were given to them. Another angel came and stood at the altar, holding a golden censer; and much incense was given to him, so that he might add it to the prayers of all the saints on the golden altar which was before the throne. And the smoke of the incense, with the prayers of the saints, went up before God out of the angel's hand. Then the angel took the censer and filled it with the fire of the altar, and threw it to the earth; and there followed peals of thunder and sounds and flashes of lightning and an earthquake. And the seven angels who had the seven trumpets prepared themselves to sound them. (Revelation 8:1-6 NASB)

As the scroll is finally unfurled, there is silence in heaven. Silence is set in contrast to the loud voice of the multitude in Revelation 7:9-10. It's a half hour of holy preparation for the unleashing of God's wrath, as if heaven holds its breath for what is about to come.

As the scroll is opened, we're introduced to the seven angels who, with their seven trumpets, unleash a horrific expression of the contents of the scroll, a series of plagues and the active judgment of God—a judgment the world has never known: hail, fire, blood, a plummeting star, blackness and the unleashing of agents of pain and suffering. It's a breathtaking visage of destruction and misery. In Revelation 9:12, John recorded the first five of the seven judgments brought about by the first five angels. He referred to these five together as the "first woe," as he warned there are yet two more to come.

The second woe is recorded in Revelation 11:14. This woe

refers to the sixth angel and trumpet that unleashes plagues and death brought by four unique angels tasked to kill a third of humanity. With their fire, smoke and sulfur, they unleash a horrific set of events on those who fail to repent, who fail to embrace the dream of God. This second woe also includes another "mighty angel" (10:1), who carries with him a judgment on the earth and sea that is so horrific that John is instructed not to write it down. This second woe includes an interesting phrase:

> Then the angel I had seen standing on the sea and on the land raised his right hand to heaven. And he swore by him who lives for ever and ever, who created the heavens and all that is in them, the earth and all that is in it, and the sea and all that is in it, and said, "There will be no more delay! But in the days when the seventh angel is about to sound his trumpet, the mystery of God will be accomplished, just as he announced to his servants the prophets." (Revelation 10:5-7)

The phrase "There will be no more delay!" refers to the immediacy and speed with which God will bring about his full and unrestrained wrath on the world—something we will see in the coming bowl judgments. The fact that there will be no delay, no intermediate steps and no reconsideration also speaks to the fact that these recorded woes are being used in a noun sense. As they occur, the woes refer to actual actions taken by God to eradicate all that's outside his great dream.

THE BATTLE BELONGS TO THE LORD

The killing of a third of unrepentant humanity is only the beginning. In the chapters to come, we see God at war with the devil, at war with unrepentant humanity and at war against a world system that relies on the commodification of peoples, the exploitation of the earth and unspeakable atrocities against God's people. God is about to go to war. And with the sounding of the last and final trumpet, he does just that, pronouncing the beginning of the end (11:15). In sounding the war cry in the seventh trumpet, God is declared victorious, and the battles that ensue are incidental. No power, earthly or celestial, can withstand God at war. God's victory is sure! Listen to the song of God's people:

> Then the seventh angel sounded; and there were loud voices in heaven, saying, "The kingdom of the world has become the kingdom of our Lord and of His Christ; and He will reign forever and ever." And the twenty-four elders, who sit on their thrones before God, fell on their faces and worshiped God, saying, "We give You thanks, O Lord God, the Almighty, who are and who were, because You have taken Your great power and have begun to reign. And the nations were enraged, and Your wrath came, and the time came for the dead to be judged, and the time to reward Your bond-servants the prophets and the saints and those who fear Your name, the small and the great, and to destroy those who destroy the earth." And the temple of God which is in heaven was opened; and the ark of His covenant appeared in His temple, and there were flashes of lightning and sounds and peals of thunder and an earthquake and a great hailstorm. (Revelation 11:15-19 NASB)

They sing that the time has come for judging, the time has come for rewarding, the time has come for destroying. Notice that it is the destruction of those who "destroy the earth."

Living in my land of woe in Inkster during those years, I was exposed to toxic, cancer-causing fumes released from the waste-disposal company three blocks from my house. During my late teens, more than eighty homeowners were involved in a class-action lawsuit against the company responsible. Many of the names we were suing were big, publically traded American companies with deep pockets.

The court battle went on for years, and from time to time, I was deposed at length. I recall sitting across the table from six lawyers representing some of the big companies. With a sneer, they questioned me for eight hours, saying that I imagined the smell, that I was making the story up to get money. I felt powerless against them in their nice suits across the glassy table. I was one of the lucky ones, however. Eventually we did settle our court case with favorable results for me and most of the others. But some of the neighbors died of cancer, and others moved away and dropped out of the battle.

I was fortunate in another way too. I lived in a country where I could bring suit against those who exploit the poor. Many exploiters, however, profit off the poor's inability to act, to defend themselves, to call into question those who "destroy the earth." Today, millions of the world's poor live downstream from toxic waste dumps where wealthy and aloof corporations pump toxins not only into the earth but also into the land and drinking water, forever destroying the farmable and usable resources of our planet. Destroying the earth is a sin against God in and of itself, but it's a double sin, for in destroying the earth, we destroy those it sustains. The poor and marginalized are at greatest risk when it comes to environmental exploitation. But as the dream of God dawns, God announces victory against the powerful, the exploiters, those who destroy the earth.

Notice also this pronouncement: "The kingdom of the world has become the kingdom of our Lord and of His Christ" (Revelation 11:15 NASB). This is one of the most significant statements in the Bible. It represents a pivotal turning point in divine history, for with the completion of the seventh trumpet, we find God finally reasserting his reign on earth. The time for grace and forbearance is over—God will now take up his rightful place as the ruler of earth.

To do that, he must first brush aside all that is antithetical to his great dream. In the next several chapters, God secures his victory over all powers—earthly kingdoms, earthly rulers, armies and world structures and, importantly, all demonic forces in their various manifestations. This pronouncement is the long-awaited pronouncement of the actualization of the dream of God, a dream that comes at a high cost.

The most striking part of this long-awaited pronouncement is the present tense "has become" in verse fifteen. In this, God's dream has begun with the seventh angel blowing his trumpet. God's dream is dawning and with it, an eradication of all that stands in its way. So holy is this moment that at the end of the pronouncement, God's temple in heaven is opened. Heaven meets earth, and earth is subsumed with the presence of heaven. With this clash comes lightning, rolling thunder, an earthquake and heavy hail. It is the collision of two worlds, the end of one time and the beginning of another.

THE THIRD WOE

The third woe is referred to in Revelation 11:14 as "coming soon." Bible scholars vary in their interpretation of the third woe, because it's not laid out in detail as the first and second woes are. The next time the word is mentioned is in Revelation 12:12: "Therefore rejoice, you heavens and you who dwell in them! But woe to the earth and the sea, because the devil has gone down to you! He is filled with fury, because he knows that his time is short."

After twenty years of considering this issue, I've come to believe that the third woe revolves around this "short" time, an intense 1,260 days of suffering before God brings an end to this present world. These 1,260 days revolve around the work of the devil and the suffering brought about by his agents. It seems odd to emphasize this number, but it refers to the last three and a half years of a seven-year period of suffering traditionally referred to as "the tribulation." The tribulation is customarily broken into two parts: the first 1,260 days and the second 1,260 days. Each is the equivalent of three and a half years when using a lunar cycle (in contrast to our customary solar cycle of 365.25 days per year). A lunar cycle was the customary way of understanding time for the Jews and is the method used when referring to the specific end-time work of Christ in Revelation.

The 1,260 recorded for us in Revelation 11:3 (the amount of time granted to God's two witnesses, who prophesy against the world during its rebellion against God), in Revelation 12:6 (the amount of time Israel is persecuted by the devil), and alluded to in Revelation 12:14 ("a time, times and a half a time"—the time Israel is protected from the persecution of the devil). This is significant for understanding this final woe upon the earth, for within it we see the duration of the woe and the central source of the woe: the devil's direct and unrestrained actions on the earth to lead humanity away from the dream of God.

Parenthetically, let me say that this kind of consideration usually turns many off to studying eschatology. When we start talking about times and dates, it seems like such a rigmarole and open to so much error and abuse. It also seems complicated and tedious. Can't we just focus on the love of God and leave all this judgment and timing up to Jesus? Many who speak this way refer to themselves as panmillennialists, joking that it will all pan out in the end. This kind of attitude toward Bible prophecy and eschatology ignores the vast volume of texts explicitly given to us to prepare us for a certain future. Ignoring or giving up on what some have argued as nearly a third of Scripture is not only lazy; it's also unchristian. We must regain a vigorous love of eschatology as the church and, in so doing, regain the fire of mission and the urgency of reaching people for Christ. There ought to be no room in Christian mission for so-called "panmillennialism," for it robs us of our passion for God's Word and end-time work to make all things new.

Can't we just focus on the love of God and leave all this judgment and timing up to Jesus? The short answer is yes and no. As followers of the dream, we focus on the great love and hope we have in Christ, the power to live the dream of God today through the Holy Spirit and the great joy that will be ours when God's dream comes in fullness. But the main question in eschatology is this: "Why did God give us a book like Revelation if it wasn't to study?" Is Revelation for future reference? Is it there to frighten us or as mere symbolism? Have the events of Revelation already been fulfilled?

These are all great questions, but they miss the primary point. Revelation is in the Bible, and the entire Bible has been given to humanity for a reason. Not one part of the Bible is an accident or is considered "additional reading." It is "God-breathed and is useful for teaching, rebuking, correcting and training in righteousness, so that the servant of God may be thoroughly equipped for every good work" (2 Timothy 3:16-17). Revelation, then, is ultimately given to us so that we can be equipped for good works in the present set of circumstances.

Sitting on my front porch in my childhood land of woe, I heard the sirens of approaching fire trucks. I could smell the unmistakable scent of burning wood. Another home was on fire. In some regards, many who live in urban poverty secretly enjoy house fires—a change in the landscape and scenery, one less boarded-up house. *I wish they'd all burn down*, I often thought. As the sirens wailed in the distance, my mind drifted to open fields of green grass, rolling over the sickness and gray. Flower petals pushed past the concrete and opened up my land of woe to the high-definition blue sky. *I wish they'd all burn down*, I thought again.

Now that I more fully understand the dream of God, I know that God's solution is not for poverty to be addressed by fire; one misery can't solve another. No, God's dream is a dream of ultimate victory, of freedom and joy. It's a dream of flourishing. To know that one day all suffering and evil will come to an end, that God has a great plan and that there is a day of reckoning and rejoicing coming, gives hope not only to withstand our current suffering but also to press into it with the power of God. God's dream is a dream for today, not just for tomorrow.

When we work to provide sustainable solutions to the complex issues facing those who suffer in poverty, we're establishing the dream of tomorrow in the lives of people today. The dream of tomorrow can be experienced today. This, in part, is why God gives us a book like Revelation—to let us know that the time of suffering has an end, the devil will be defeated and Christ will reign victoriously.

A COUNTERFEIT DREAM

This third and final woe revolves around God's indirect judgment on humanity through letting the devil do his worst. While the devil now is able to traverse between our world and heaven, in the last days, he will be cast out and unleashed on earth as a form of judgment from God (Job 1:6; Jude 1:9; Revelation 12:9-10). God's grace currently restrains the powerful works of the devil on the earth. Paul referred to the restraining work of the Holy Spirit in preventing the devil from having his way with the world:

And now you know what is holding him back, so that he may be revealed at the proper time. For the secret power of lawlessness is already at work; but the one who now holds it back will continue to do so till he is taken out of the way. And then the lawless one will be revealed, whom the Lord Jesus will overthrow with the breath of his mouth and destroy by the splendor of his coming. (2 Thessalonians 2:6-8)

As the devil is "revealed," he goes on to deceive the world, to destroy God's people and to attempt to create a counterfeit dream. God's dream is a dream of flourishing and freedom, of joy and justice for all people, but the counterfeit dream is one of war, bondage, coercion and suffering.

The devil gave his power to two great "beasts," and we read,

The beast was given a mouth to utter proud words and blasphemies and to exercise its authority for forty-two months. It opened its mouth to blaspheme God, and to slander his name and his dwelling place and those who live in heaven. It was given power to wage war against God's holy people and to conquer them. And it was given authority over every tribe, people, language and nation. All inhabitants of the earth will worship the beast—all whose names have not been written in the Lamb's book of life, the Lamb who was slain from the creation of the world. (Revelation 13:5-8)

Interestingly, the number 1,260 is referenced here again in the form of months. Forty-two months on a lunar cycle is exactly 1,260 days. This beast is allowed to rule as the physical manifestation of the devil for this "short time" before the end. Notice what this beast commits itself to doing. It wages war against God's people and exercises authority over "every tribe, people, language and nation." This is a key phrase in God's dream for all people, and it is included here to mark just how closely the counterfeit dream of the devil mimics God's dream. The unfortunate reality is that, in the last days, the whole earth will worship this beast and therefore, indirectly, the devil who empowers it. In the end, the devil gets all he has been after since the beginning—rule over God's creation and being worshiped as God.

THE ACTUALIZATION OF THE DREAM

We draw this chapter to a close, not with the devil on his throne, but rather with the victorious appearance of Jesus. The three woes have a set time and place. As the devil's time comes to an end, as the final woe closes, we see the return of Jesus: "Then I looked, and there before me was the Lamb, standing on Mount Zion, and with him 144,000 who had his name and his Father's name written on their foreheads" (Revelation 14:1).

While there is still quite a bit left after this verse, from here forward we read of the victory of the war-waging Jesus, the Lamb who comes to slay the wicked, rescue his people and bring an end to the rule of the devil. We see nothing but victory—no more delay but swift and unrelenting action on the part of God through the end-time judgment of Christ. The seals have been broken, the scroll has been unfurled, the trumpets have sounded, and now Jesus returns. It's time for the actualization of the dream of God, beginning with the eradication of all that is antithetical to God's great dream.

In Revelation 14, we find one last act of grace on God's part. An angel flies over the earth with the "eternal gospel," the message of God's grace, and it is sent again to "every nation, tribe, language and people." The message this angel brings is to "fear God and give him glory, because the hour of his judgment has come. Worship him who made the heavens, the earth, the sea and the springs of water." The angel says, "The hour of his judgment has come" (Revelation 14:6-7).

Christ will now execute the final judgment before the new world dawns and God in his grace extends an invitation to all: worship him who made the heavens and earth. This stands in stark contrast to the counterfeit dream of the devil, where all the peoples of the earth worship a beast who rises out of the earth and sea (Revelation 13:1-11) instead of the true God, who made both earth and sea. A second angel follows and announces that Babylon—the city that represents the false dream of humanity—has fallen.

A third angel follows, announcing judgment on all who worshiped the beast, saying, "They, too, will drink the wine of God's fury, which has been poured full strength into the cup of his wrath" (Revelation 14:10). Recall the image of the cup of God's unrestrained wrath in chapter four. Christ "drank" God's full, unrestrained cup of wrath intended for the world. In the garden of Gethsemane, before going to the cross, where he received the full wrath of God, Jesus said, "My Father, if it is possible, may this cup be taken from me. Yet not as I will, but as you will" (Matthew 26:39). The cup he referred to is the same cup about to be poured out on the earth in Revelation 14 and following. Interestingly, when Christ is on the cross, just prior to his death,

> Knowing that everything had now been finished, and so that Scripture would be fulfilled, Jesus said, "I am thirsty." A jar of wine vinegar was there, so they soaked a sponge in it, put the sponge on a stalk of the hyssop plant, and lifted it to Jesus' lips. When he had received the drink, Jesus said, "It is finished." With that, he bowed his head and gave up his spirit. (John 19:28-30)

Jesus' pronouncement of thirst on the cross is his ultimate response to his Father, who asked him to drink the cup of his wrath on behalf of all humanity. A jar of wine vinegar was given to Christ, symbolically representing the full, unrestrained wrath of God. Christ is the sole possessor of this wrath until it will be "poured out" on all the world in preparation for the long-awaited dream of God (Revelation 15).

Drug addiction, violence, disease, prostitution, prison— these realities accessorize the everyday reality of the urban poor. My city of woe could have been any place in the world where such realities cloud a vision of another world. Smoke and toxic fumes choked out hope, looming signs extinguished dreams, but the reality is that God's dream can come to such places of despair. God's dream is breaking into the nightmare and with it the hope of a world to come.

In this world, followers of our dreaming God fight an ongoing battle against suffering, poverty and injustice, but in the end, all will be made new. We live in an era of grace, and though things are often terrible, God's good news is available to all, because Christ drank the cup of God's wrath on our behalf.

God's dream found me in a dirty place, a place of bondage and misery. God's dream found me and turned my life upside down. This dream, anchored in a time to come, can change not only our lives but also the entire world. God's dream is not a dream of past actions. As we've seen, as important as Christ's work on the cross was, God's dream is anchored in the future work of Christ. When Christ appears as a conquering warrior, one able to pour out the wrath of God because he is the possessor of that wrath, he comes to establish the dream (Revelation 14:1). God's dream is anchored in the certitude of Christ's work, which will make all things new.

This certain work of Christ enables us to dream with God,

for without the just and final judgment of Christ, there is no foundation to our commitment for a just world, no alleviation of suffering and no belief that the world could one day be something other than what it is. Only the end-time work of Christ provides the foundation for our commitment to justice and action, the foundation for our work toward establishing the dream of God in our time.

11

God's Great City

• • •

Wow! It's Christmas," she said, gently stroking the Christmas tree with both hands. Reaching up and down, she unfurled her arms wide, as if to embrace what she considered to be Christmas—dangling ornaments, gold tinsel, silver ribbon, sparkling lights. It all seemed magical to my newly adopted two-year-old. "Wow! It's Christmas!"

For Gabriella, the concept we had been trying to explain was subsumed in one object—the Christmas tree. We gathered around to marvel and laugh at her simple and infectious joy. Kiren and Addison knew better; they had been around the Christmas block a few times. They knew that Christmas meant Christmas cookies, strolling in the downtown park with a warm cup of Starbucks, painting pottery with Mom and, most of all, presents. Lots and lots of presents. But Gabriella's full, brown lips pressed together tightly each time she repeated "Wow!" and then, bursting forth, she exclaimed louder and louder, "It's Christmas!"

There's something profound in my daughter's embrace of the tree and misunderstanding of the totality of Christmas at the age of two. While Christmas is more than the traditional holiday tree, overwhelming joy and infectious sense of wonder capture the true Christmas spirit. There's no way my two-year-old at her first Christmas as a Moore could fully understand our family traditions or the meaning of the decorative symbols we've used to educate our children about Christ's first coming. So great and awesome is the story of Christmas, we are left speechless. It is, as they say, the most wonderful time of the year, and our attempts to unpack the significance of Jesus' coming to earth can never express the wonder of the event.

I believe the end of God's story will be just as difficult to comprehend. The magic of Christmas begins with Christ coming to us, invading our world, dispelling darkness with light. The magic of the end of the story revolves around us going to be with God, allowing his world to invade our hearts, shedding our darkness to be at home with the Lord.

AT HOME WITH GOD

In preparation for his departure from earth, Jesus said,

> My Father's house has many rooms; if that were not so, would I have told you that I am going there to prepare a place for you? And if I go and prepare a place for you, I will come back and take you to be with me that you also may be where I am. You know the way to the place where I am going. (John 14:2-4)

In the end, we go to live with God, to dwell with him in a unique place he has prepared for his people. It's a fantastic notion, living in God's house. What is God's house like?

During Christmas, I love to sleep over at my in-laws' home. Though they live just fifteen minutes from my own warm bed, there's something special in letting go of my sense of control and drifting off in their guest bed. I love having my kids wake up at Grandpa's house with the smell of bacon and eggs. The mess my kids make doesn't seem to bother me at my in-laws' house; the noise that typically makes my hair stand on end goes almost unnoticed. It's a warm place of comfort, relaxation and fun. Is that what God's house is like? While I hope that God's house has some aspects of my in-laws' home, I don't think I can make that comparison any more than we can equate a tinsel-clad tree with the true glory of Christmas.

Going to live with God—now, there's an idea. My slave ancestors sang, "Soon-a will be done a-with the trouble of this world . . . troubles of the world, trouble of this world . . . soon-a will be done a-with the trouble of this world . . . going to live with God!"[3] After their exploitation, the sale of their children, the rape of their mothers, hope of justice and a home of their own kept my people going. Living with God is the great hope contained within the dream of God. It is the culmination of all the aspirations of our hearts and the pinnacle of God's purposes for us.

As the great divine story of history draws to a close in Revelation 21–22, we see this emphasis reiterated over and over again. The enemies of God are thrown into the lake of fire and Satan is forever expelled from God's world.

> Then I saw a new heaven and a new earth, for the first heaven and the first earth had passed away, and there was no longer any sea. I saw the Holy City, the new Jerusalem, coming down out of heaven from God, prepared as a bride beautifully dressed for her husband. And I heard a loud voice from the throne saying, "Look! God's dwelling place is now among the people, and he will dwell with them. They will be his people, and God himself will be with

them and be their God. He will wipe every tear from their eyes. There will be no more death or mourning or crying or pain, for the old order of things has passed away." He who was seated on the throne said, "I am making everything new!" Then he said, "Write this down, for these words are trustworthy and true." (Revelation 21:1-5)

In verse one, the emphasis is on newness—a new heaven, a new earth. John wrote that the first heaven and first earth had "passed away." In reference to death, mourning, crying and pain, he again said in verse four that "the old order of things has passed away." The passing away of the first heaven and first earth indicates the total destruction that occurred with the great apocalyptic events of the tribulation. The passing away of the old order of things, the way the world used to work, indicates just how radically different the actualization of God's dream from the world we know now. The world to come is not just a refurbished version of the world we know now. It is altogether new.

This does not mean that there will not be elements of our world that "make it through" to the next. In fact, Andy Crouch points out in *Culture Making* that the new creation will be filled with elements of the old: "it seems clear from Isaiah 60 and from Revelation 21 that we will find the new creation furnished with culture. Cultural goods too will be transformed and redeemed, yet they will be recognizably what they were in the old creation—or perhaps more accurately, they will be what they always could have been."[4] The old gives way to the new and within the new creation we see the world as it always should have been!

In making all things new, God makes things as they were meant to be, as he originally desired them to be. This is particularly true for relationships: our relationships to one another, the world, and most of all to God himself. What is most breathtaking about this new world and what should cause us the greatest sense of awe and wonder is the fact that we live with God and that God lives with us. In verse three, a loud voice announces that God's "dwelling" is "among the people," that he will dwell with us and we will be his people. What will this place of dwelling, of face-to-face communion and celebration, be like?

In answering this question, we are like a two-year-old enamored with the twinkling lights of an artificial tree. What ability do we have to comprehend such wonder? When I ask my twelve-year-old what he thinks of heaven, he usually says, "Well, I hope we can fly!" My nine-year-old adds, "We'll be able to eat all the carbohydrates we want!" This comes from a girl who has been tormented by a father who does all the cooking in the house and has been living on the Atkins diet for over eight years. So, sugar and personal levitation—pretty low expectations for heaven.

The adult versions of our expectations are no less flawed than our children's visages of heaven. Many imagine weight loss or a restoration of a youthful body, adventures where there's no fear of death or pain, limitless feasting or continuous relaxation. More serious visions include reunion with loved ones, answers to questions, freedom from crushing circumstances or making peace with enemies. Whether serious or silly, none of these expectations fully grasp the greatness of the world to come. Nothing I could ever write could either.

What we do know, however, is that the most consistent and awe-inspiring aspect of the world to come is the fact that it will be lived *with God*. God says, "I am making all things new." The most significant aspect of this newness is the reality of living with God—something lost in the garden, partially restored in the coming of Christ but fully realized in the new world to come.

NOW JUST STAY WITH ME: WE ARE
WHERE GOD DWELLS

The description of the dwelling place of God seems to move back and forth between an actual, physical place and a description of God himself and God's people. The interchangeability of the dwelling place with the person of God and the people of God is so seamless that it's often confusing as to whether there is an actual, literal dwelling place. But both are true. The dwelling place of God is both a real place and a relational state between God and his people. This is often what's so confusing about the study of eschatology. Many of the details given in the Bible about future events, figures, dates and realities have multiple dimensions, sequential or simultaneous fulfillment, and literal as well as figurative meaning. This is most true when it comes to the dwelling place we will enjoy with God.

John saw a new heaven and earth, and within this vision, he also saw a holy city coming down from heaven from God. He referred to this holy city as the "new Jerusalem" and compared it to a "bride adorned for her husband" (Revelation 21:2 NASB). Undoubtedly, this city refers partially to the people of God, those who have chosen to follow the great dreamer of all time. The wedding supper of the Lamb is a celebration of the final reunification of God's people with their groom, Jesus Christ. Thus, this city that comes down from heaven refers to the people of God who are adorned through the righteous work of Christ on the cross, making her ready to be united to her husband.

Paul referred to this unification: "For this reason a man will leave his father and mother and be united to his wife, and the two will become one flesh. This is a profound mystery—but I am talking about Christ and the church" (Ephesians 5:31-32). This reference to the unification of a man with his wife has its ultimate fulfillment in the unification of Christ and his people.

In verse 31, Paul referenced Genesis 2:24, where we read about the first marriage, which is the archetype for all marriages: "For this reason a man will leave his father and mother and be united to his wife, and they will become one flesh." Genesis 2 and Ephesians 5 point to the moment when finally the bride and groom are brought together to dwell together in a face-to-face relationship, recorded for us in Revelation 21. *The people of God are synonymous with the city of God.*

Further evidence of this is found in the other direction, in this understanding of the people of God as a city.

> I am coming soon. Hold on to what you have, so that no one will take your crown. Him who overcomes I will make a pillar in the temple of my God. Never again will he leave it. I will write on him the name of my God and the name of the city of my God, the new Jerusalem, which is coming down out of heaven from my God; and I will also write on him my new name. (Revelation 3:11-12)

This promise to the church at Philadelphia is a promise to all "victorious" Christians. It indicates that the victorious will be made pillars in God's temple, a part of the actual structure of the dwelling place of God and that they will never leave God's presence. They will have written on them God's name *and* the name of the city—new Jerusalem—which comes down out of heaven from God, just as we saw in Revelation 21. Undoubtedly, this heavenly Jerusalem refers to the people of God being given to her groom, Jesus Christ, at the end of time.

A RELATIONAL REALITY

Most of us don't think of reality in terms of relationship, but God does. God defines reality primarily on the basis of relationship. We see this in Revelation 21–22, where we learn a great deal about God's vision for the place where his dream will be experienced. This dwelling place, this temple, this house—the city of God—is also a real place.

In Revelation 21:12-21, we are given details about the city's measurements, the materials that are used in its construction and information about its gates and walls. The details of the city are too precise to be thought of as merely symbolic. Within this passage, we again see the seamless interchangeability of the city with the people: "The wall of the city had twelve foundations, and on them were the names of the twelve apostles of the Lamb" (v. 14). In this verse, we see that not only does God write on the people the name of the city, but the city itself has written on it the names of the people—in this case the twelve apostles. This indicates that this city is a real place as well as a people, the people of the dream.

Here are ten additional breathtaking details about the city of God:

1. It has no temple, for its temple is the Lord God the Almighty and the Lamb (21:22).

2. It has no need for the sun or moon, for the glory of God is its light, and it has the Lamb as a lamp (21:23; 22:5).

3. It is open to the nations and will be the perpetual place of homage for the people of the nations and the kings of the world to pay tribute (21:24, 26).

4. The gates of the city will never be shut (21:25).

5. There will be no night there (21:25; 22:5).

6. Only clean people and things will enter the city, only those written in the Lamb's book of life (21:27; 22:3).

7. There will be a river with life-giving water coming from the throne of God and the Lamb (22:1).

8. There will be a street (22:2).

9. There will be a tree of life, bearing healing fruit for all the nations (22:2).

10. There will be face-to-face celebration and worship of God (22:3).

This place of God's dwelling is so intertwined with God himself and God's people that the place and the relationship become somewhat indistinguishable. The primary point in understanding God's new city is that it revolves around relationship. This is the basis on which God defines reality.

More important than what the gates are made of or whether or not the street is paved with gold is the fact that we will be there, that we will see God face to face. It is a place of peace, of safety and security, and of abundance. Far from my city of woe and still farther than the aspirations of all the great cities of our world, the city of God stands unique throughout divine history. It is a unique city, for the city itself is subsumed in the fact that it is where heaven meets earth, where God and God's people are finally united. It is the dream of God come to life—in real time and a real place.

God's great prize has never been a geopolitical state, or temples made of gold, or the religious sacrifices of women and men. The living God has been after a living city throughout divine history—living stones with living walls and living gates set atop living streets. God has been about building a living city, and in his dream, we see this city coming down from heaven, prepared by God as his own dwelling place. On the mountain of God, we see the city of all time, the living city, coming down as a bride made ready for Christ—the climax of God's great dream for himself and for the world.

Understanding this, we see how cheap was the substitute the

devil used to tempt Christ in Matthew 4:8-9: "Again, the devil took him to a very high mountain and showed him all the kingdoms of the world and their splendor. 'All this I will give you,' he said, 'if you will bow down and worship me.'" What mountain could be higher than the end-time mountain of God? What kingdom could be greater than the end-time kingdom of God? What splendor, what reward coming up from the earth and from the hands of the devil could ever be greater than the heavenly Jerusalem coming down from heaven?

The devil attempted to bribe Christ with nothing more than the baubles of this world in exchange for his own bride. Christ was undeterred from the great dream of God and the great prize of the city of God set on the mountain of all time.

12

The Dream of God and Mission

● ● ●

Shards of gray poured like snow from the mound of clay. My dad always sculpted with a squinty eye and a cigarette dangling from the left of his lips. I would sit silently, legs crossed under the table where beauty was born, just happy to sit with my dad as he created worlds out of clay.

In his sculptures, he brought forth life and purpose. My dad's creations always seemed to be born out of a mixture of passionate determination, a longing for beauty and a secret inner violence. His sculpting tools were more than artist's instruments; they were weapons of warfare, tools that willed his creations into being. His weapons destroyed chaos, decimating the gray-green solid mass on that table as he willed it into a transcendent expression of life.

Overjoyed to play some small part in this warfare, I would sweep up the shavings and chunks of clay each day for him to use again. He never wasted the shavings, always reusing them to cast his thoughts into existence. Day after day, sculpture after sculpture, order emerged from chaos, beauty came from ugliness, and transcendent meaning soared from fallen shards of clay.

If you know an artist, you know what I'm talking about. You know the willing of chaos into order. The transformation of nothingness into beauty. The bringing forth of a dream that lives only within the mind's eye.

There is often eccentricity in the lives of artists, with a cost to themselves and to those around them. We children of artists may have wanted for food and clothing, but we never wanted for blocks of gray-green dreams. My dad's commitment to his art came before all things. He was sold out to it.

This image of the willful, determined artist may not be too far from the beautiful biblical image of divine mission. God is on mission to resculpt our world, to recreate out of the fallen chunks a new world. The sculpture of God's first creation lies in ruins; shards of clay litter the floor below where beauty and transcendence once stood. Our world is not the world God intends, so we engage in mission.

Throughout this book we've looked at the importance of God's end-time judgment, and there is now no greater response to what we've learned than the consideration of our actions. Our mission, the work of joining God in what he is doing, is our ultimate response to eschatology—not charts and graphs and escapist plans. Christian mission born out of a deep conviction of Christ's return is mission with the power to change the world and our own lives in the process. Mission is not merely modifying the world in which we live. Ours is not the work of pressing out the wrinkles of life, of giving a nice little religious boost to the lives of those we seek to reach. God's mission is to make all things new. In pursuing this mission, we see the radical commitment God makes to achieve his goal. God is determined, above all else, to resculpt the world and establish an everlasting kingdom of joy.

Ours is the privilege of joining with God in establishing his reign where it is not present. It is an end-time work that brings the dream of tomorrow into the nightmare of today. Our mission is about joining God in making all things new.

THE NEED FOR MISSION

Whenever we witness times of suffering and injustice, we are reminded of the need for mission. Exploitation, abuse and neglect, death and disease, destruction and displacement—the sufferings we witness in this world cause us to dream of another one. Suffering and injustice causes some people to lose faith, to doubt the existence of a world other than this one. But others have confidence in the reality of another, better world, and it motivates them to put their lives on the line. It inspires great acts of bravery and heroism; it drives them to give their all to reach for the dream. History is filled with the stories of millions who hoped against hope for another world and who risked their lives to establish justice in their pursuit of joy.

The dream of God includes us—our efforts, our passions and our risks—to establish his dream where it is not. The dream of God is not merely a future reality. It is a reality that we can taste, touch, feel and live today if only we would reach for it together. Throughout the history of the church, this has been the foundation of biblical mission.

The founder of the International Justice Mission, Gary Haugen, has inspired me to reach for the dream. At InterVarsity Christian Fellowship's Urbana 2000 mission conference, I sat listening to Gary talk about slavery. He did not speak of the slavery of my people, of some abstract historical memory. Gary introduced me to the horror of the modern-day slave trade. I had no idea that slavery existed in our time or that there were people giving their lives to free slaves or prosecute their captors.

As Gary spoke, God got a hold of my heart, and I wept through most of his short message. He spoke of the forced prostitution of children, of the exploitation of the powerful and of what a courageous faith in Christ must look like in light of such atrocities. In one brief message, Gary changed my life. His message was the flashpoint for what I call my second conversion.

My faith journey began after I came to Christ as an atheist philosophy student at the University of Michigan in the late 1980s. My childhood home had a sign on the front: "The Moores, The Atheists." We had a barrel beside our house for burning Bibles and other religious propaganda.

I had experienced the power of the person of Christ during an attempted suicide on Christmas Eve of 1989. On that night, Jesus Christ miraculously saved me from the brink of death, and I was persuaded that God loves us and is at work to save us—all of us. From that experience in 1989 until Gary's message in 2000, I had one singular focus: to reach as many people with the gospel as I could. Sharing the hope of Christ with lost people was and continues to be my mission. But at Urbana 2000, something happened—a conversion within my conversion.

My heart broke as I faced a crisis of faith. Weeping in my seat at Urbana, I experienced the heart of God for those who suffer the hell of this world. I realized my gospel and my vision of Christ were too small. I asked myself through tears, "How can my Jesus not only save sinners from the hell to come? How can he save them from the hell that is now?" If it was true that there were millions of people living as commodities, that there were children being locked in dark rooms by the thousands to be raped for pay, how could my Jesus do anything about their plight?

Before Urbana 2000, for the first time I held my great-great-grandfather's slave papers in my own hands—government papers that documented his slavery. Burrell Avery was the property of a Kentucky slave owner. He was insured like cattle, recognized as such with the approval of the state and federal government. He served in the "Colored Army" on behalf of the U.S. government, and when he died, his family got absolutely nothing. My heritage as an African American is one of subjection and servitude.

I remember weeping that night at Urbana with these two images in my mind: the image Gary painted of modern-day slaves and the image of Burrell's suffering. As the worship band came to the stage, I stood and said to God in a quivering voice, "If you were able to free my people from the last great global tyranny, you must be able to free those slaves today." Ever since this declaration, this sinner's prayer of my second conversion, I have invested my life as an abolitionist, seeking to mobilize resources for frontline organizations in their fight against modern-day slavery. I have played a small part in championing their cause, in encouraging them in our fight for justice, and along the way God has made my heart new.

Thanks to the courageous work of Gary Haugen and the International Justice Mission, I left the auditorium that night born again, again. Until that point, I had been sure that Christ saves sinners, but after hearing Gary speak, I was persuaded that Christ is out to save the entire world.

Reaching for the dream is what we've been left on the earth to do. When we reach for the dream, we actuate in our time and space a piece of what will come in fullness at the end of the age. Gary and the International Justice Mission are not merely creating a picture of the dream of God, but a beachhead of its coming. Gary's message that night was an invitation to a dream: the dream of justice, the dream of restoration, the dream of hope—the dream of God. That dream is at the heart of every great missional vision, the launch of every true church, the birth of all great organizations. The dream of God fuels all true mission. As we join God in bringing his dream to the world around us, we join the great historic mission of the church.

There are many obstacles to mission and to this dream. Our world is broken in so many ways. Children die in countless numbers from diseases that are treatable or preventable for lack of medicine that the wealthy can obtain at any corner drugstore. Poverty and greed form a vicious cycle, and often the children of the world's poor pay the ultimate price. Currently, more than two thousand children under five die from malaria each day—that's one child every forty seconds. Malaria kills nearly one million people each year; 85 percent are children under five. Each year an estimated 250 million people get infected with malaria. That's equal to 83 percent of the U.S. population. Malaria is the fourth leading cause of child deaths worldwide and second leading cause of child deaths in sub-Saharan Africa. The poorest of the poor suffer most.

Slavery, death from disease, displacement, hunger—we know this is not the way things are supposed to be. So we long for another place, a place of hope. Yet there is so much more after the child is saved from a life-threatening disease, after the girl is rescued from the brothel and the hungry family is fed. Remember, God's dream ends in flourishing.

THE POWER OF HOPE, THE DREAM OF JOY

For several decades in my city, Detroit, hope was all but lost. Detroit was the murder capital of the United States in the 1980s. Often, however, when we lose hope, something seems to drive us to seek it out. Now there are many in Detroit who dream again. There are corporations and government officials, teachers and civil servants, business leaders and scholars who know the secret of Detroit's rich heritage. There is a sense of purpose and drive, a renewed sense of entrepreneurialism and innovation. Detroit is alive with hope. But this is not the first time.

During the nineteenth century, at the height of slavery, when all hope seemed lost, countless slaves in the South heard of a city of hope. The dream of freedom had a name: Detroit. For many slaves who escaped from the Deep South, this city, the Detroit River—with freedom in Canada beyond it—was a dream that inspired them to risk their very lives. For scores of abolitionists and slaves alike, Detroit was the destination of hope.

The trek along the Underground Railroad, a system of safe houses and safe people, led escaped slaves to Detroit—for many, a year-long journey of over a thousand miles. This trek was fueled by the hope of freedom, opportunity, safety and, most of all, joy. The dream of joy is at the center of the heart of every woman, of every man. Often it's the goal behind the goal, the greater dream of a thousand aspirations. For countless slaves, it fueled prayerful miles and expectant singing. Their dream may have started with the longing for freedom from the injustice and suffering of slavery, but there was something behind that dream.

What do we do when justice and freedom have been obtained? We live the life we were meant to live. This is the dream that is beyond justice—the dream of joy. Slaves would sing of the Jordan River, speaking figuratively of crossing the Detroit River into Windsor, Canada, finally being free of fear and the repercussions of their escape, which were often death or dismemberment.

For many of my ancestors, slavery was all they knew. They were born into the slave system, often separated from their parents and shipped off to fields throughout the South. They never knew the dream of freedom. So what is it in the heart of a woman that dares to dream of a world she knows nothing of, a world without rape or exploitation where she is free to choose her loved ones and run her hands through the hot, dense July air? Where does the dream of a boy come from, a dream of a fantastical world of play, when all he's known is the work of slavery? I believe the quote of an unknown slave says it all: "All my life I been called a slave. They tell me I belongs to my master. That may be true about my body, but my soul remembers a time when I was free, so when I get a chance I will run."[5]

THE MISSION STATEMENT OF THE DREAM

I believe our soul remembers this dream because we're made in the image of God. Like dusty light, this dream pokes and peeks into our world of injustice and suffering and connects powerfully with our soul, because it is the world we were made for, a world of joy. Nothing else will satisfy our longing in this world for the next. Nothing else will do.

All of humanity longs for this dream, whether we are conscious of it or not. Millions have risked their lives and are still risking their lives so the dream can come to pass.

A dream can literally change the world, as we see with the dream of Gary Haugen or Dr. Martin Luther King Jr. We often use the concept of a dream to refer to a wish, a desire or a hope. Real change, however, comes through conviction, passion, power and action. During the civil rights era that brought real and lasting change to millions of African Americans, it was the dream of one man coupled with the real actions of Whites, Blacks, Asians, Latinos and others that brought that dream to pass. During this current movement of activists and abolitionists, it is the dream of people like Gary that spurs microfinance enterprises and multinational cooperatives, causes women and men to move across seas to work with the hurting and at risk, and changes the course of would-be affluent and powerful attorneys and politicians for the cause of justice. Dreams are powerful.

Dreaming is not incompatible with action; in fact, a dream of real substance, conviction and vision requires action. This is why mission exists instead of mere dreaming. We can't wish the dream of God to pass. God invites us to pursue it. This is why the church exists.

When Jesus launched his ministry, he used the missional words of an ancient prophet to do so. With these words, he launched not only his public ministry but also the inauguration of the coming of the dream of God. We read these words of declaration in Luke:

> He went to Nazareth, where he had been brought up, and on the Sabbath day he went into the synagogue, as was his custom. He stood up to read, and the scroll of the prophet Isaiah was handed to him. Unrolling it, he found the place where it is written: "The Spirit of the Lord is on me, because he has anointed me to proclaim good news to the poor. He has sent me to proclaim freedom for the prisoners and recovery of sight for the blind, to set the oppressed free, to proclaim the year of the Lord's favor." Then he rolled up the scroll, gave it back to the attendant and sat down. The eyes of everyone in the synagogue were fastened on him. He began by saying to them, "Today this scripture is fulfilled in your hearing." (4:16-21)

Jesus purposely found these words in the scroll and read them, but what he did that had never been done in any synagogue by any reader was to declare that these words were being fulfilled by their reader. He announced the dream of God in his reading. Through Isaiah, Jesus declared that the dream had begun with the coming of the Spirit of God, who enables the good news to be proclaimed to the poor, freedom to be given to prisoners, the blind to be restored, the oppressed to be set free and the year of God's grace to begin. Let's consider each of these for a moment, because they form the foundation of all mission and the contours of the dream of God.

GOOD NEWS FOR THE POOR

Jesus says that the Spirit's work within him enables him to proclaim the good news to the poor. The proclamation of God's good news as we see throughout the Bible revolves around the work of Christ, his death, his resurrection, his rule and his return to judge the living and the dead.

We see this throughout the first church in Acts. In the first postresurrection sermon, recorded in Acts 2, Peter announced the same dream of God as Jesus did in Luke 4. In this passage, we see Peter proclaiming Jesus Christ as crucified (v. 23), raised from the dead (v. 24), the rightful Lord of all (vv. 25, 29-35) and the one who will judge the nations. In this last regard we read,

> I will show wonders in the heavens above and signs on the earth below, blood and fire and billows of smoke. The sun will be turned to darkness and the moon to blood before the coming of the great and glorious day of the Lord. And everyone who calls on the name of the Lord will be saved. (Acts 2:19-21)

With these words, Peter added to the announcement of Christ by pointing out that it is not only the good news of God's grace that is being offered to humanity, but also the warning of his dreadful judgment to come. We also read in verse forty, "With many other words he warned them; and he pleaded with them, 'Save yourselves from this corrupt generation.'" The proclamation of the good news is always an expression of God's grace and mercy as well as a warning of the certainty of his coming justice.

However, what made the announcement of Christ so significant was the fact that it was to the poor. The poor are at the heart of mission because their poverty is an expression of evil, of brokenness; it is antithetical to the dream of God. Poverty is almost always the product of greed, lust, selfishness and fear (forms of self-worship). As the good news of God's dream goes to the victims of self-worship, God imposes his rule against all false gods who hold their victims hostage in poverty.

FREEDOM FOR PRISONERS

In Christ's announcement of the dream of God, he points out that there is freedom for the prisoners. In a Western culture where false and unjust punishment is rare, we struggle with wanting prisoners to go free. We want prisoners to be punished, to serve their time—and occasionally we want them executed. However, throughout history and in many places in our world today, many are imprisoned for a variety of unjust reasons—for standing up against evil, for being poor, for being the "wrong" ethnicity, for being female.

The concept of *prisoner* globally is more often related to exploitation rather than justice. Prisoners are frequently victims of others' greed, lust, selfishness and fear (again, self-worship). In releasing those who have been imprisoned, God imposes his rightful rule over all false gods who victimize the marginalized and powerlessness, who are held hostage to their worldly power.

SIGHT FOR THE BLIND

Christ inaugurates the dream of God's coming by proclaiming sight for the blind. The blind are frequently incapable of caring for themselves, of defending themselves, of holding jobs or negotiating their physical surroundings. The blind are often poor, often oppressed, often excluded from building wealth. In Jesus' time, they were seen as doubly cursed by God. People thought their blindness was a form of God's judgment.

In announcing the dream of God as sight for the blind, Christ not only corrected this theological error but also expressed God's love, grace and mercy for the "least of these" and God's intent to correct their handicaps. Medical infirmities are an expression of a world that is not right, a world that is antithetical to the dream of God. In God's dream, people are not lame or sick; they do not lack the bodily capabilities God intended for all people. In God's dream, the handicapped and infirm are made complete.

In the church's mission, we see the centrality of both medical mission and healing. The church seeks to bring healing and wellness to all who are sick and handicapped. Either in this world or the next, that mission will be complete. When God's dream breaks into the nightmare of this world, it comes with the power to heal, either supernaturally or through the sincere and loving expression of the medical sciences.

THE OPPRESSED SET FREE

Christ inaugurates the dream of God's coming by setting the oppressed free. We do not have to be physically bound in an institution of punishment to be imprisoned. The oppressed today are in a unique form of prison and need to be set free. They are victims of others' greed, lust, selfishness and fear. They are the girls of brothels, the boys of brick kilns. The oppressed are the farmers who farm lands that do not produce enough to feed their families—just enough to pay their government officials or landlords. The oppressed are those who, through urban poverty, lack of infrastructure and educational opportunities, have little or no hope of bettering their circumstances.

The oppressed are not merely poor; they are worse off—they are victimized in their poverty. In their need, they are exploited out of others' self-worship. By setting these people free, Christ announces the evaporation of the power of all false gods who hold the poor in chains. Though their circumstances may not immediately change, by pledging allegiance to Christ, the oppressed are set free. Jesus' pronouncement is not figurative but sets forth the unstoppable force of the dream of God that will one day be actualized. We read in Revelation that, as God's dream comes to pass with the great judgment of the city of Babylon,

> the merchants of the earth will weep and mourn over her because no one buys their cargoes any more—cargoes of gold, silver, precious stones and pearls; fine linen, purple, silk and scarlet cloth; every sort of citron wood, and articles of every kind made of ivory, costly wood, bronze, iron and marble; cargoes of cinnamon and spice, of incense, myrrh and frankincense, of wine and olive oil, of fine flour and wheat; cattle and sheep; horses and carriages; and bodies and souls of men. (18:11-13)

In this description of mourning over the judgment of the great city Babylon, we see the commoditization of human beings sold as slaves, and so we see the root of all oppression.[6] Oppression is always, at its core, an act of commoditization, because it uses people as the solution to a desire to acquire power, status, possessions or security. Oppressed people are those who have been treated as the solution to someone else's greed and selfishness. By setting the oppressed free, God imposes his rightful rule over all souls as the one who owns us all and alone has the right to determine our worth.

THE YEAR OF THE LORD'S FAVOR

Finally, Jesus proclaims the year of the Lord's favor. The concept of the "year of the Lord's favor" can be traced back to the Israelite's year of jubilee, a divinely established year of societal redistribution that was to occur every fiftieth year. In Leviticus, we are introduced to God's intention in this yearlong celebration:

> Consecrate the fiftieth year and proclaim liberty throughout the land to all its inhabitants. It shall be a jubilee for you; each of you is to return to your family property and to your own clan. The fiftieth year shall be a jubilee for you; do not sow and do not reap what grows of itself or harvest the untended vines. For it is a jubilee and is to be holy for you; eat only what is taken directly from the fields. (25:10-12)

This year was a year of freedom, a time when property went back to the original clan to prevent usury, oppression, manipulation and radical inequality. Just as important, however, was God's intention to give land, animals and his people a yearlong rest and to have them enjoy only what grew naturally without work. God loves rest; God loves peace; God loves joy and celebration. In this we see the heart of his dream. It is not a dream of mere sustenance and justice; it is one of celebration, where all things flourish.

In the year of jubilee, we see that God's dream comes when we are able to experience joy in its fullness. A lack of joy and celebration often comes as a result of greed, lust, selfishness and fear. In establishing seasons of grace, redistribution, joy and celebration, God usurps the power of self-worship. Nothing can corrupt or take away the joy that comes with jubilee. Jesus' announcement begins an era of grace—an endless epoch of the jubilee of God.

The final judgment will obliterate all that stands in the way of jubilee, and Revelation 22 describes what the eternal jubilee of God looks like for all peoples:

> Then the angel showed me the river of the water of life, as clear as crystal, flowing from the throne of God and of the Lamb down the middle of the great street of the city. On each side of the river stood the tree of life, bearing twelve crops of fruit, yielding its fruit every month. And the leaves of the tree are for the healing of the nations. No longer will there be any curse. The throne of God and of the Lamb will be in the city, and his servants will serve him. They will see his face, and his name will be on their foreheads. There will be no more night. They will not need the light of a lamp or the light of the sun, for the Lord God will give them light. And they will reign for ever and ever. (vv. 1-5)

In the announcement of the dream of God in Jesus' first public message, we see the end of time. We see God's dream unleashed on a world of pain and suffering. In this, we see the foundation for all mission, a dream that is beyond justice, beyond salvation, beyond rescue. We see restoration and flourishing. And in the end we see joy.

13

A Dream
Beyond Justice

• • •

In 2010 I spent ten days in Cape Town, South Africa, at the Lausanne Congress on World Evangelization. When I wasn't in sessions, I walked the city, gave food out to the homeless, conversed with artists at the local marketplaces and went on a tour of the region. I've never been to a place of such beauty. I've also never seen such abject poverty alongside such immense wealth. Cape Town is home to one of the largest garbage slums in the world, with an estimated one million people living in a post-apartheid, garbage-based city.

As I drove past a portion of this sprawling, exploding mass of humanity, I saw children playing in dirt, huts with no electricity and young men with clothes three sizes too big. On the other side of the road were Lamborghinis, well-dressed and well-fed people touring the vineyard hills just off the beaches, and Whites riding on horses along the ocean's edge.

What was most stirring was the difference in the faces between the super rich and the super poor. The high degree of drug addiction, HIV/AIDS and malnourishment made the poor in South Africa look almost like a different species of humans. But you know who the rich looked like? They looked like me.

Even though I come from poverty, I come from American poverty. No matter what our circumstances are in the United States, we are a part of the world's wealthiest and most privileged. God used that trip to rebreak my heart for the poor and to remember what God has delivered me from, because poverty is an evil, but one day God will make even this place new.

MORE THAN JUSTICE

All history is heading somewhere. It is driving toward a place beyond justice—a place of joy. Deep down, we know this at the core of who we are. God is in the process of making all things new, of bringing about his great dream of another world.

Unlike us, with our hopes and aspirations, God is fully capable of bringing about his plans. His vision and passion for another world are coupled with his power and will to accomplish his dream. God's dream will come to pass, and the exciting part is that it includes us, our actions, our faith and our longings.

Some wonder why God doesn't just snap his fingers and bring about his dream right away. God invites us to join him in setting things right, in helping the world around us in both small and big ways to begin to look the way it is supposed to be. In the Revelation of John, God gives us a glimpse of the day he will bring his dream to pass:

> And I heard a loud voice from the throne saying, "Look! God's dwelling place is now among the people, and he will dwell with them. They will be his people, and God himself will be with them and be their God. 'He will

wipe every tear from their eyes. There will be no more death' or mourning or crying or pain, for the old order of things has passed away."

He who was seated on the throne said, "I am making everything new!" Then he said, "Write this down, for these words are trustworthy and true." (Revelation 21:3-5)

God could make the dream come alive instantly, but this wouldn't be good for everyone, or even most. His dream is not only of another world of beauty, order and joy. It is also of severe consequences, particularly for those who have put their faith and trust in a world that is incompatible with his dream. Making all things new is not good news for all.

We need to realize that there is a dream behind our dream, a longing behind all our aspirations, that we can seldom put our fingers on. Our dream is a dream beyond justice—a dream rooted in another place. Our soul remembers this place because we're made in the image of God. The dream of our heart is anchored in the eternal dream of God. This is beyond justice.

The reality of suffering and injustice causes most people to experience what the Bible calls "holy indignation." Indignation is that "strong displeasure at something considered unjust," or "righteous anger."[7] There is something holy about righteous indignation; it brings out the best in humanity. Emerson wrote, "A good indignation brings out all one's powers."[8]

If you are like most people, as you see the suffering and injustices of the world around you, you long to do something, to be an agent of transformation. Kevin Jenkins, president of World Vision International, expresses this holy indignation this way:

We don't accept that any child should have to go to bed hungry. We don't believe that mothers should watch their children get sick and have no way to help them. We don't believe that fathers should work sixteen hours a day and still not be able to provide for their children. We don't believe teachers should give lessons to children who have no textbooks, paper or pens. We don't believe governments and rebels should recruit youths to kill, or that girls should be bought and sold, or that parents must sell their children to pay their debts. . . . There is a righteous anger at the heart of World Vision. But at the same time, we overflow with love for all those with whom we are called to serve.[9]

Indignation causes us to reach for the dream, to band together across racial lines, across economic lines, across religious lines to do something greater, something that none of us could possibly do alone. The realities of injustice and suffering cause a deep sense of dissonance and even rage within us. This rage at the injustices and suffering of others demonstrates that we are made in the image of God.

The commoditization of people is as old a practice as civilization itself, but God will reverse this in what the Bible calls the kingdom of God.

THY KINGDOM COME

The kingdom of God is a reality where the deepest longings of our hearts for justice and abundance are fulfilled, because God will be in control instead of corrupt governments, greedy corporations and broken systems of law. The kingdom of God is synonymous with the dream of God. It is in this kingdom dream where we can feel the density of the warm air as it flows between our fingers and the green grass beneath our feet.

Throughout the Bible, God gives us glimpses of a world that is barely imaginable with the world as it is today. In Revelation, God gives us a horrific glimpse of the judgment that will come to those who exploit the poor and the world's resources, and those who traffic in human beings. We read about the future destruction of a city of sin, where people make their fortunes from the exploitation of the poor. Though the city is referred to as Babylon, it represents every city where evil is allowed to flourish. Listen:

> The kings of the earth will see the smoke of her burning, and they'll cry and carry on, the kings who went night after night to her brothel. They'll keep their distance for fear they'll get burned, and they'll cry their lament: Doom, doom, the great city doomed! City of Babylon, strong city! In one hour it's over, your judgment come! The traders will cry and carry on because the bottom dropped out of business, no more market for their goods: gold, silver, precious gems, pearls; fabrics of fine linen, purple, silk, scarlet; perfumed wood and vessels of ivory, precious woods, bronze, iron, and marble; cinnamon and spice, incense, myrrh, and frankincense; wine and oil, flour and wheat; cattle, sheep, horses, and chariots. And slaves—their terrible traffic in human lives. Everything you've lived for, gone! All delicate and delectable luxury, lost! Not a scrap, not a thread to be found! (Revelation 18:9-14 *The Message*)

In the dream of God, we see his great anger and wrath; we see divine, holy indignation in action. Many people have a hard time with a God portrayed as vengeful, who would bring destruction to people and places, who would judge the world. After all, isn't God supposed to be loving? When we consider that men will fly across seas to commoditize young boys and girls and that people pay to rape children, the question shouldn't be, "How can God punish the world?" but rather, "How can God *not* punish the world?"

God is loving, and his dream is rooted in joy and freedom. But he is also holy and pure. It would be a nightmare, not a dream, for the world to continue as it is today without a course correction.

According to the U.S. Department of State, an estimated 50 percent of all trafficking victims are children under the age of eighteen. Every year 1.2 million children are trafficked for child labor; another million are trafficked for sexual exploitation. Every day, millions of children live the nightmare, not the dream. God hates injustices, and he cares deeply for the hurting and the poor; this is what authentic religion is all about.

And this is why our dream is a dream beyond mere justice. The things that cause us anger do so because we are made in the image of God. In his dream, God will make all things new. All history is heading toward this cosmic collision, a day when God will judge evil and bring an end to injustices and suffering. In Revelation, we read of this day of judgment:

> And there were loud voices in heaven, saying, "The kingdom of the world has become the kingdom of our Lord and of His Christ; and He will reign forever and ever." And the twenty-four elders, who sit on their thrones before God, fell on their faces and worshiped God, saying, "We give You thanks, O Lord God, the Almighty, who are and who were, because You have taken Your great power and have begun to reign. And the nations were enraged, and Your wrath came, and the time came for the dead to be judged, and the time to reward Your bond-servants the prophets and the saints and those who fear Your name, the small and the great, and to destroy those who destroy the earth." (11:15-18 NASB)

As we have seen, all history is heading toward a cosmic collision, a time of great punishment and wrath against the perpetrators of evil, those who victimize the poor, who enslave the weak and exploit the world's resources while indulging in every luxury known to humankind.

ON EARTH AS IT IS IN HEAVEN

The dream of God is not a far-off, ethereal idea; it is coming to pass right now, all over the world—particularly in some of the toughest situations. The kingdom of God is not merely a place and a time in the future. It is showing up and transforming our world. For years after encountering Gary Haugen's message of courageous faith at Urbana 2000, I sought to raise money and mobilize donors for the International Justice Mission (IJM). I frequently highlighted IJM's work in Cambodia. In 2011, I was given the opportunity to travel to Cambodia and spend a significant amount of time at IJM's field office in Phnom Penh.

During my tour of the office, the field director took me to a small, interior office. A nearly shut door hid a man just finishing a phone call. The field director introduced him: "This is our chief investigator. Nearly all of our prosecutions of perpetrators in country are in some way, shape or form owed to this man's hard work." The man looked at the ground as if embarrassed by this high praise.

I felt as if I were in the presence of royalty. In a near-hidden room in a hidden field office in a forgotten country was a person known by God, a hero in the kingdom and an agent of the dream. How many young girls and boys owed their lives to this man without knowing it? How many dreams would grow from their release? What worlds would be unleashed through the actions of their freedom? All these thoughts and emotions swirled inside me in a moment of introduction that seemed to hang in the air forever.

I couldn't think of anything to say or ask, so I laid my hands on his arm and prayed, "God, use this man to continue to unleash your kingdom in the lives of those who suffer. Protect him from the enemy, and give him joy in the work you have called him to. Use him to bring the good news of Jesus Christ to those locked away in darkness." Shortly after this prayer, I left IJM's office and vanished down the street, back to my hotel and eventually back to my life in the United States. But this man continues to work in the army of the Lord, bringing the good news of release for the captives, establishing God's dream of the future in the lives of Cambodians.

The kingdom of God begins with the good news of Jesus Christ. All history is heading toward the day when Jesus Christ will reign, when he will set all things right. But the good news of Jesus is that it has already begun. He declared the kingdom of God as a present reality in his first public address: "The Spirit of the Lord is upon me, because he anointed me to preach the gospel to the poor. He has sent me to proclaim release to the captives, and recovery of sight to the blind, to set free those who are oppressed, to proclaim the favorable year of the Lord" (Luke 4:18-19 NASB). From this point forward in history, the kingdom of God has been advancing toward God's dream.

Notice Jesus's emphasis on the poor, on those in bondage, on the sick and the oppressed. Justice is God's heartbeat, and the kingdom of God revolves around making all things new. When Jesus told his followers to go and preach to the cities of his day, he told them to heal the sick and to announce, "The kingdom of God has come near to you" (Luke 10:9 NASB). God's kingdom dream has always revolved around good news to those who need it most. This is the mission of the followers of Jesus: to announce the good news of the kingdom of God and to invite the nations to join in the dream.

The dream of God is realized only through the person of Jesus Christ. When we think of an eight-year-old who has been sold by her mother in Myanmar to an international sex tourist for two hundred dollars or of a father who would sell his son as a bonded laborer in India to bake bricks, we see what kind of evil we are up against. In the state of Ohio alone in 2010, there was an estimated one thousand U.S.-born children, most under the age of fifteen, sold as prostitutes.[10]

We can legislate against such realities, prosecute those who traffic in the flesh of children and build aftercare facilities for victims. But without addressing the hunger that gives rise to such a rape of humanity, we are failing to be holistic in our approach to evil. Ultimately, injustices always trace back to spiritual brokenness, to soul sickness. Real evil exists in our hearts and in the world around us, and that requires real spiritual power to address.

IN CHRIST ALONE

This is why we need the power that comes only through the person of Jesus Christ. In the life and death of Jesus, we hear the echoes of another world, a world where couples stroll, laughter flourishes and the streets hum with music. When Jesus died on the cross, he dealt once and for all with evil in the world and the evil in our hearts.

As Jesus hung on the cross, his death paid the full price for all the things we've done and all the things we've left undone that are incompatible with the dream of God. We are not just victims in this world or neutral observers of the world's suffering. We have all contributed to the wreckage of the world in many ways. Jesus' death on the cross enables us to begin again and to experience God's forgiveness.

The Bible also tells us that Jesus returned to life on the third day—he was raised from the dead. And the power that raised Jesus from the dead is available to us today. The spiritual life we find in the person of Jesus is given to us who would follow him as kingdom agents, proclaiming and demonstrating the kingdom to the world around us. God's dream advances as God's agents—Jesus' followers—take the power of God and apply it to the broken places, to the people who are suffering and to our own lives.

THE END OF THE STORY

Divine history is going somewhere. All that God is doing points to another time and place, culminating in the grand dream of God. In contrast, human history can be summarized as the rise and fall of our pursuit of a dream we were made for and its vicious counterpart, the nightmare of injustice and suffering. What does God's dream look like in its fullness? What picture does Jesus give us of this coming kingdom?

In the book of Revelation, we get a vivid snapshot of God's dream fulfilled. We are introduced to a city unlike any city we've ever seen or read about. American cinema and literature have done us a disservice by giving us images of heaven as a place where we'll lounge partially nude on clouds, feeding from clusters of grapes while eternally honing our harp-playing skills. But the dream of God revolves around a city where infrastructure and agriculture are intertwined; a city where beauty and order thrive alongside population density and activity; a city of purpose and pleasure. This city that we read about stands in diametrical opposition to the city of Babylon we read of earlier. It is also the antithesis of our cities today.

The following words about God's heavenly city have long fueled those who follow Jesus in the church's mission, calling us to reach for the dream:

The twelve gates were twelve pearls, each gate a single pearl. But there was no sign of a Temple, for the Lord God—the Sovereign-Strong—and the Lamb are the Temple. The City doesn't need sun or moon for light. God's Glory is its light, the Lamb its lamp! The nations will walk in its light and earth's kings bring in their splendor. Its gates will never be shut by day, and there won't be any night. They'll bring the glory and honor of the nations into the City. Nothing dirty or defiled will get into the City, and no one who defiles or deceives. Only those whose names are written in the Lamb's Book of Life will get in. (Revelation 21:21-27 *The Message*)

Then the Angel showed me Water-of-Life River, crystal bright. It flowed from the Throne of God and the Lamb, right down the middle of the street. The Tree of Life was planted on each side of the River, producing twelve kinds of fruit, a ripe fruit each month. The leaves of the Tree are for healing the nations. Never again will anything be cursed. (Revelation 22:1-3 *The Message*)

In this city of hope, we see a river of life and a tree of healing, offering abundance and restoration. God's dream is a dream beyond justice, though it includes the judgment necessary to establish it. Notice in this description that nothing dirty or defiled can get into the city. It is a holy place. God's dream goes beyond holiness and beyond justice; it is a dream of flourishing.

I think of the hope of the slaves in the Deep South who dreamed of Detroit. Even at the height of its grandeur, Detroit had only a shadowy resemblance to the city of God. It was never the final destination of slaves. They dreamed of something better, and that dream behind their dream fueled their journey. New York, Vancouver, Beijing, Buenos Aires, Dubai—

all these and many other great cities hold aspects that are alluring to us. Beauty, transcendence, natural treasures, the arts, fashion, abundant resources, power—all these things are attractive to us because our soul remembers. In the dream of God, realized through the person of Jesus Christ, we see the culmination of divine history in the city of God.

As the unknown slave said, "My soul remembers a time when I was free, so when I get a chance I will run." What does it mean to respond to the dream, the world we remember? I believe this unknown slave has the right answer—we run! The dream God has put in our hearts is really an invitation to pursue something greater than ourselves, greater than the façade around us. It is an invitation to run toward the dream.

REFLECTING THE HEART OF GOD

How do we make the dream a reality? How do we respond to the dream God has for the world and for each of our lives? How do we sustain our commitment to actualizing God's dream for justice?

We choose to pursue the dream, to join countless slaves, countless missionaries, countless dreamers who followed the Chief Dreamer. This is the only way we can personally and corporately realize God's dream. When we choose to pursue the dream, we choose to follow Jesus, who sets the pace and the direction for the dream. We learn from him and submit to his way of thinking and doing. As a result, we begin by living a more active faith—we see our lives differently and join a purpose bigger than ourselves. The reality is that Jesus is already setting the pace and giving your life direction if you are truly following him.

For those who follow Jesus, the path looks as unique as each person. Though mission is always heading toward God's dream, there is a unique portion of the path God has for each of us. We see small glimpses of this calling in our longings, the particular aspects of God's dream we long for most. What dream has God placed on your heart? The passion and drive you have and the joy you find are likely indicators of where the kingdom of God is touching your soul. It might be tutoring children living in poverty in your own backyard, helping to right the wrong of modern-day slavery, helping end a preventable disease like malaria in your lifetime or something else that God has placed on your heart. Where do you see this other world tearing at the fiber of your soul? The invitation God is making to you now is to be more like Jesus and to pursue a world that's more like God's kingdom than the world of pain, suffering and injustice you see.

Pursuing this world requires conditioning. Just like runners condition their bodies in pursuit of a goal, God invites us to condition our heart. He wants us to begin to see the way he sees the things he cares about.

There is something beyond justice and its joy. There is a place our soul calls out for, a place our soul remembers. Our response to God's invitation begins when we imagine a life of joy, of endless summer nights, peace, safety, security—and most of all, togetherness. God longs to restore the world, and that will come to pass in a final way one day. But today he invites us to run with him in bringing the kingdom of God to our world. Our response to God's invitation is to run toward this place of magic, to breathe in, to dream with God and to join him in making all things new.

14

Joining God in
Making All Things New

• • •

Faces pressed against glass, waiting for loved ones, business associates, clients and friends—hundreds shared the steamy night air outside the Phnom Penh airport. Smiles and waves, tears and laughter spread like a contagion as passengers exited after this last flight into Cambodia. Buses and cabs jockeyed for the exit and down the street toward the heart of the capital city.

I was unprepared for what I was about to experience. While sending money to Phnom Penh for nearly ten years, I always thought the city would be entirely poor, decimated by the recent history of war, displacement and genocide. But what I saw was a city in revolution—a revolution of success. In many ways Phnom Penh is an emerging world-class city, with shiny buildings reaching for the sky, a brand-new airport, the ubiquitous presence of multinational conglomerates and, most importantly, the hope of success in the eyes of the Cambodian people.

Day after day, getting in and out of tuk-tuks in Phnom Penh, I was struck not so much by the abject poverty, the meat pots that lined the streets or the presence of obvious places of prostitution, but rather by the excitement and sense of expectation in the Cambodian people.

Cambodia has a shot at the big time, a shot to give her people what has been elusive for so many generations—a taste of a better life, a new world. Angry Birds and Hello Kitty backpacks, glistening smartphones and fine clothes accentuate this sense of hope in the university districts where over one hundred thousand Khmer (Cambodian) students are getting a taste of this new world. Driving their own motos (in the U.S. we call them "mopeds"), these emerging leaders of a rebirthed nation represent new wealth, new knowledge and new hope for a land that just a few short decades before saw the decimation of millions in the killing fields and death camps, particularly those who had achieved any kind of educational status. In short, Phnom Penh is alive with a sense of hope and destiny.

However, the presence of success and hope stood in stark contrast to the other side of the story. Everywhere I went, I was exposed to the public nudity of impoverished children, the places of branded debauchery, the stench of unsanitary conditions and the intimation of harsh classism. It was apparent that this "new world" had not come to all the Khmer people.

In fact, this new world of hope came with an entirely different set of realities for many who were paying the price of success. I visited villages on the outskirts of the bustling city and witnessed people who had been forcibly displaced by land developers, large groups of people living atop polluted waterways and large swaths of land that used to be vibrant lakes, all dried up to make way for the progress of the city. I heard horror stories of organ trafficking and harvesting, and the exchange of children for antiviral medications. It is apparent that in the new Cambodia, what was new for some was not good news. For many, it is a nightmare of suffering, injustice and exploitation.

ALL THINGS NEW

God's dream is to make *all things* new in a way that causes all the earth, every people and every thing, to flourish to the glory of God. Mission is the work of joining God in bringing this dream to pass in the present in anticipation of the future. When we join God in making all things new, we establish that future, permanent, eschatological reality that all will enjoy.

When the dream of God breaks into our lives and our world, it creates something permanent, something that will not be displaced in the world to come. When a church, a campus ministry or a community outreach center is planted, God's dream is rooted in the present but extends into the future. When a well is dug, a school is built or an orphanage opens its gates, the dream of God becomes actualized in our time.

Of course, this doesn't mean that all human-initiated activism is of eternal value or even earthly good. Frequently, the efforts of people produce new problems, further exploitation or more injustices. For example, in the past, well-meaning people have sought to fight slavery by purchasing slaves. This approach is as ancient as slavery itself. Unfortunately, this often creates a higher demand for slaves, which causes traffickers to secure more supply. In fighting slavery, we often create more slavery.

In less overt ways, however, activism is often nothing more than another self-serving expression of human idolatry that leads not only the activist astray but also those they seek to help. By giving the appearance that we can solve the enduring and complex needs of the world through our physical strength, our intellectual prowess, our money and resources, and our organizational sophistication, we create an idol of self-reliance that is as damnable as the poverty, exploitation and suffering we seek to address. No lasting change can come without the unique power that only God wields. No cheap substitute of the dream of God will ever satiate the human heart or solve the lasting problems of the human race. Only the end-time work of Christ can do this.

God's dream is a dream to make *all things* new, not some things for some people. God's dream is a dream of total renovation. And we can play a part in that right now.

FILLING THE NEW WORLD

In our younger years, my wife and I had a house built, which took about eight months. During this time, we lived in a small room on the second floor of my in-laws' house. Our furniture, our artwork and various home accessories were all in storage. Our new home was almost twice the size of the one we had sold. So we knew that though we had plenty of "stuff," it wasn't enough stuff to fill our new home. We visited art shops and furniture stores as we had means, with the hope of preparing to fill it. We found a painting here or there, picked out a new kitchen table, a new couch. When the big day finally came to move into our house, we brought all our old and new fineries into our home.

After a few weeks of emptying boxes, hanging shelves and moving furniture in, our reaction was, "Why does our house feel so empty?" There were paintings and places to sit in some rooms, but other rooms stood empty.

I believe the work we do in helping to make all things new in our world today is like trying to fill the new world. It is an impossible chore, and we will never have enough time or resources to build and fill the home to come. God has been doing the work of filling his house, his city, his new world since this world was infected by sin. In his house, there will be nations and peoples from every time; every era will be represented. We often think about the ethnicities that will fill God's new world, but we often don't consider other types of differences. People from every time and place, from every nation and race, will fill God's world.

The good news is that the work we do under Christ today has lasting, permanent impact on the "rooms" of the world to come. When we join God in making all things new, we fill his future city with citizens; we fill his streets with the sound of happy children; we open the doors and windows of real hope and opportunity for those who suffer today. Like the servants who go into the highways and the hedges, we announce to the world that God's dream is coming to pass as we work under Christ, as we join him in his work to make all things new.

> And He who sits on the throne said, "Behold, I am making all things new." And He said, "Write, for these words are faithful and true." Then He said to me, "It is done. I am the Alpha and the Omega, the beginning and the end. I will give to the one who thirsts from the spring of the water of life without cost." (Revelation 21:5-6 NASB)

In the end, only he who sits on the throne can lay claim to "making all things new." We don't make anything new by ourselves; only through Jesus Christ can we change the world around us. However, it's a solid truth that biblical mission is the work of God's people joining him in his endeavor. That is, we are actually participating in making all things new as we join his mission. What we do on earth not only changes circumstances in heaven and not only changes the eternity of those we impact—it changes the physical space of the world to come as well. Recall the symbiotic nature of the city that comes down out of heaven with the people of that city: change the people, and you've changed the city of God, literally.

TRANSFORMING HEAVEN AND EARTH

When we preach the gospel, disciple new believers or engage with hurting people, we are working with the power to change the world. And change the world we will. But which world? Both worlds! We not only change earth through our partnering work with God, we also change heaven itself. The power of the good news of Christ changes all worlds. It is the very means by which the kingdom of this world becomes the kingdom of our Lord and of his Christ. The power of Christ is the wonder-working power to transform today into tomorrow.

What artwork occupying the city streets of God's dream is a direct result of the faithful acts of Christian women? The women who preached Christ in the factories of London during the industrial age have literally altered the landscape of the world to come. What tributes to God's glory stand as sculpted edifices to this wonderworking power in the lush parks and thoroughfares of the city of God? The men who gave their lives as martyrs in places like Malaysia or Kenya have caused God's city to shine and to extend his praises to eternity.

No act in Christ's name is lost on the city of God. No sacrifice on the part of Christ's bride will be overlooked. The world to come is filled with the actions of all God's people in every generation. Planting and establishing that kingdom is a forever act, one that can't be reversed and one that will fill the world to come with wonder and praise to God.

This is what's at stake in Christian mission—the very world to come. When we join God in making all things new, we are participating with God in the end-time work of Christ. Christian mission is nothing less than an eschatological act

done on the part of an eschatological community with eschatological ramifications for eternity. Of this, we can be certain.

Perhaps this is what Paul referred to when he wrote these
words:

> According to the grace of God which was given to me, like
> a wise master builder I laid a foundation, and another is
> building on it. But each man must be careful how he
> builds on it. For no man can lay a foundation other than
> the one which is laid, which is Jesus Christ. Now if any
> man builds on the foundation with gold, silver, precious
> stones, wood, hay, straw, each man's work will become
> evident; for the day will show it because it is to be revealed
> with fire, and the fire itself will test the quality of each
> man's work. If any man's work which he has built on it
> remains, he will receive a reward. If any man's work is
> burned up, he will suffer loss; but he himself will be saved,
> yet so as through fire. (1 Corinthians 3:10-15 NASB).

Paul said his work as an apostle extended the kingdom of
God. He then warned that each person must be careful in
building. His warning was twofold. First, he said we can't build
on any other foundation except the person of Jesus. Dream-
building work requires an eternal foundation rooted in the
past, accessible in the present and extending into the infinite
future. Jesus is the foundation for the dream and the only way
for us to join God in making all things new today. No amount
of Western moralizing, religious sentiment or humanitarian
good intentions can establish the foundation for the city of
God. Only Christ can do this.

Second, Paul warned that a testing of fire would show what
kind of building we do. Those who work with the best of all
they have—gold, silver, precious stones—remain and have a

reward. Work done with the leftovers, the refuse, the after-thought—wood, hay, straw—will burn, and there will be no reward. Paul was quick to point out that he was not speaking about salvation, but about what is lasting and contributes to the dream of God. He said that those who build with perishable materials will suffer loss in the test of fire to come, but they themselves will be saved. Their work will either last or be consumed. This day and the associated testing with fire speaks of the Christ-event Paul spoke of:

> God is just: He will pay back trouble to those who trouble you and give relief to you who are troubled, and to us as well. This will happen when the Lord Jesus is revealed from heaven in blazing fire with his powerful angels. He will punish those who do not know God and do not obey the gospel of our Lord Jesus. They will be punished with everlasting destruction and shut out from the presence of the Lord and from the glory of his might on the day he comes to be glorified in his holy people and to be marveled at among all those who have believed. This includes you, because you believed our testimony to you. (2 Thessalonians 1:6-10)

When Jesus is revealed, he will be so in a blaze of fire, coming down from heaven with powerful angels. Jesus spoke of this Christ-event several times, as recorded in the Gospels (Matthew 16:28; 24:27; Mark 8:38; Luke 21:27; John 1:51).

In the 2 Thessalonians passage quoted above, Paul said Jesus will punish those who do not know God, who do not obey the gospel of Jesus, and they will be punished with "everlasting destruction"—shut out from the presence of the Lord *and* the glory of his might or power. In citing the punishment to befall humanity, Paul spoke both of the destruction that comes with the unrestrained wrath of God and the implications of being excluded from the presence of God, from God's transforming power.

In making all things new, the end-time work of Christ reestablishes a face-to-face relationship with God. Recall that for God, all of reality is ultimately a relational reality. The new world is most noted as being the place where we experience God's real presence (Revelation 21:3). The new world is made possible because of the glory of God and the might of his power, as Paul stated and as Revelation 21 assures us. There is no light, no life, no water, no food, no safety in the world to come that does not directly come from God himself. This is the result of the might of his power to be unveiled in the coming world. A large part of the destruction and punishment that those outside Christ will experience comes from the fact that they will be forever removed from the light, life, safety and sustenance found in Christ's presence.

From girls who dance in the glare of red lights to leaders in the highest places of government, those outside of Christ are damned. People are lost without Christ. Most Western evangelicals would like to ignore this fact. Nevertheless, Paul said that when Christ appears in blazing fire, he will punish those who do not know him or obey him—actively as well as by implication of their being banished from the glory of his might.

We know that the wonderworking power of Christ changes the whole world, not only people's lives. But in this day of global activism, I want to be very clear that *Christ's focus is on saving people*. People are the centerpiece of God's dream. When Christ went to the cross, when he shed his blood in the Jerusalem sun, he did so to save people from the destruction to come.

What does it mean to join God in making all things new? We could list dozens of ways in which we can and should respond to God's end-time work. I would like to recommend three courageous ways we can join God in his end-time work today—proclaiming the good news, doing good works and reading Scripture aloud—though this is far from an exhaustive list.

PROCLAIM THE GOOD NEWS

The first way we can respond to God's dream to make all things new is to bring his re-creative power to people who are lost, who do not know Christ and who do not obey his gospel. After all, this is the instruction Jesus gave to us as the end of one time gave way to this end-time age we now live in:

> All authority in heaven and on earth has been given to me. Therefore go and make disciples of all nations, baptizing them in the name of the Father and of the Son and of the Holy Spirit, and teaching them to obey everything I have commanded you. And surely I am with you always, to the very end of the age. (Matthew 28:18-20)

This last great command should be understood holistically. We can't reduce this command to evangelistic preaching. In making disciples of all nations and teaching them to obey everything Christ commanded, we have the basis for anti-trafficking work, care for AIDS and malaria patients, food for the hungry, clothing for the naked, release for the prisoners. All of this is included in global discipleship.

However, *the mission of the church is never anything less than the proclamation of the good news of Christ.* This is what we saw the first church do in Acts—they proclaimed Jesus. They also shared meals and property and resources as those among them had need. They challenged political and religious powers. And they set the precedent for all medical mission and humanitarian efforts in their care for the sick and poor.

There is no false dichotomy in the Bible between the

preaching of Christ and the practice of justice and compassion. But in our age, the latter threatens to eclipse the former. We are in danger of repeating the same error that many of the great mainline denominations made: give up on the proclamation of the gospel in exchange for nothing more than human activism.

The first way in which we need to respond to the end-time work of Christ is to proclaim the message of forgiveness Christ prayed from the cross. We see this up until the very end in Revelation, as the angel of the Lord flies through midair with an eternal gospel, calling the nations to "fear God and give him glory, because the hour of his judgment has come. Worship him who made the heavens, the earth, the sea and the springs of water" (Revelation 14:7). This gospel is preached to the entire world as a final act of God's grace. From the ascension of Christ in Matthew 28 until this angelic sermon of repentance in Revelation 14, the gospel of God's grace and forgiveness stands at the center of all divine and ecclesiastical mission. We must preach Christ. As Paul said of himself, "Yet when I preach the gospel, I cannot boast, for I am compelled to preach. Woe to me if I do not preach the gospel!" (1 Corinthians 9:16).

DEVOTE YOURSELF TO GOOD WORKS

The second way in which we need to join God in his end-time work is to fill the world to come with good works. We have been created for good works: "For it is by grace you have been saved, through faith—and this is not from yourselves, it is the gift of God—not by works, so that no one can boast. For we are God's handiwork, created in Christ Jesus to do good works, which God prepared in advance for us to do" (Ephesians 2:8-10).

The reason we've been created and then re-created by Christ is for good works. What are good works? Certainly preaching Christ, sharing him boldly with lost friends and relatives, neighbors and coworkers is a good work. Good works also entail caring for the real, temporal needs of people, not as a mere means to then preach Christ, but to bind up, to restore, to release, to fill others with joy and to cause women and men everywhere to give glory to God.

Good works don't bring us to God; they make those already connected to God closer to him. Good works don't make us good; they do not save us from sin, death or hell. Good works are the evidence that God has made us good and that his grace has saved us. Good works are the evidence of a person being transformed from the inside out.

Good works are both simple and complex. A cup of cold water in the name of Jesus, visiting prisoners, sharing food and giving money to the poor—these are all simple expressions of good works. Every Christian, no matter what her station in life, is required to engage in these simple acts. They are small ways in which the world to come breaks into the world that is now.

Good works are also complex. They are long-term commitments, strategies, career trajectories, life sacrifices and more. They include things like moving into an urban context to build relationships with the poor, making a lifelong commitment to an adopted daughter, erecting buildings where medicine and food can be distributed, and building organizational coalitions that can do far more together than they can apart. Good works can and should entail high-level plans and commitments to spreading God's dream to everyone in every place. This requires much more than vision, talent, charisma or money; it requires the supernatural power of God.

In joining God in doing good works, we must connect with him through prayer. Prayer touches everything. We can't preach Christ—we can't even perform the simplest of good works with any meaning—unless we are connected to God in prayer.

Mother Teresa, so noted for her impact through simple service, knew this well:

> Just once, let the love of God take entire and absolute possession of your heart; let it become to your heart like a second nature; let your heart suffer nothing contrary to enter; let it apply itself continually to increase this love of God by seeking to please Him in all things and refusing Him nothing; let it accept as from His hand everything that happens to it; let it have a firm determination never to commit any fault deliberately and knowingly or, if it should fail, to be humbled and to rise up again at once—and such a heart will pray continually. People are hungry for the Word of God that will give peace, that will give unity, that will give joy. But you can't give what you don't have. That's why it is necessary to deepen your life of prayer.[11]

Mother Teresa spoke of both *the source* of our spiritual energy and motivation in our good works and *the way in which we access* such godly energy and motives: through connecting with God in prayer. Prayer in evangelism and prayer in good works, both simple and complex, is how we invite heaven to invade earth and join God in making all things new.

We often hear the phrase "We don't change things through prayer; prayer changes us." I don't believe this is true. While we are transformed from the inside out through prayer, I believe that through praying, children of the new world access supernatural power, opening a portal from another world into our own. When we pray, we open a window of light into darkness, we expel the disease of moral decay, we engage spiritual forces, and we contest the world powers of our day. Prayer both changes us and changes our world.

READ THESE WORDS ALOUD

I recommend one final way in which we can join God in making all things new. It's so simple, so seemingly benign that I fear you may brush it aside in light of the more obvious suggestions of evangelism and good works. I want to assure you that this recommendation can be just as powerful as prayer-filled evangelism and good works. I recommend that Christians everywhere return to the ancient practice of publically reading the words of Scripture aloud.

Reading God's words out loud in public places, not just in the members-only buildings we call church, is one way we can unleash the power of heaven on earth. We see this throughout the Scriptures. Moses read the Book of the Law as a part of establishing the covenant (Exodus 24). Joshua read "all the words of the law" to the people (Joshua 8:3). In 2 Kings 22, Shaphan found and read the book of the law, and this reading played a pivotal role in bringing revival to Israel. Most notably, Ezra read the Book of the Law from daybreak until noon to all the people, reestablishing the covenant and ushering in a time of great revival (Nehemiah 8).

In the New Testament, we see this practice continued as well. Jesus launched his public ministry in a synagogue as he read aloud the scroll of Isaiah (Luke 4:16-20). It was the common practice of the Jewish people to read Scripture in their meetings, a practice adopted by the first church.

We also see this in Paul's instructions to Timothy: "Until I come, devote yourself to the public reading of Scripture, to preaching and to teaching" (1 Timothy 4:13). In Paul's mind, reading the Scripture was equal to preaching and teaching. Yet how often do we find local congregations "devoted" to reading Scripture publicly? Reading aloud the words of Scripture has historically been a practice of the church, but in the West, it has nearly disappeared.

In the book of Revelation, reading aloud is pivotal. Not only do we see the end-time work of God roll forth after each segment of the scroll of the Lamb is read and declared, but the entire book itself was given to the church with the intent to be read out loud. In the beginning of Revelation, we are told,

> The revelation from Jesus Christ, which God gave him to show his servants what must soon take place. He made it known by sending his angel to his servant John, who testifies to everything he saw—that is, the word of God and the testimony of Jesus Christ. Blessed is the one who reads aloud the words of this prophecy, and blessed are those who hear it and take to heart what is written in it, because the time is near. (Revelation 1:1-3)

In these end times, part of discipling the nations is to teach them everything Christ has commanded. We do this through preaching, teaching and publicly reading God's Word. God intends his words to be declared, and reading the actual words of Revelation and the Bible in general is one way we declare God's dream.

THE TIME IS NEAR

God's intention in giving us the book of Revelation was to reveal to us what must "soon take place." At the end of the book, John was told, "Do not seal up the words of the prophecy of this scroll, because the time is near" (22:10). Revelation is given to us *because* the time is near. This is the opposite of large parallel passages of Daniel that also portray the end-time work of Christ. Daniel was told, "Go your way, Daniel, because the words are rolled up and sealed until the time of the end" (Daniel 12:9). Christ has ushered in the end-time work of God, and so the scroll is open. After Christ ascended into heaven, he sent the Holy

Spirit to empower the eschatological community, the church. As the church now permeates the earth, heaven has come to stay.

We live between two worlds: the world of the now and the world that is to come. But the most exciting thing is that both worlds are connected. What happens in one world impacts the other. All divine history is moving toward a cataclysmic conclusion, one where these two worlds collide. In this collision, we see Jesus in his full glory.

On our way toward the revelation of Jesus at the end of time, we are invited by God to join him in making all things new, to renovate our current world and to fill the world to come. We fill God's house, his great wedding hall and the banquet table when we engage the world around us with the power of the gospel, doing good and bringing the dream of God to the world. We open a portal between the two worlds, allowing the world to see heaven standing open and the Lamb on his throne.

This vision of a world to come is the foundation of all Christian mission. In it we see the ultimate fulfillment of all that has gone before—the birth of nations, the rise and fall of Israel, the incarnation of Christ, his brutal death, his glorious resurrection and the filling of the church at Pentecost by the Holy Spirit. Every moment of the divine story points to what is revealed in Revelation 21, where God makes his home with us, where we become his people and sit down at the marriage supper of the Lamb. All history is pointing toward that climactic moment when the one seated on the throne says, "It is done! I am the Alpha and the Omega, the Beginning and the End," to that moment where at long last, "the kingdom of the world has become the kingdom of our Lord and of His Christ" (Revelation 21:6; 11:15 NASB).

In pursuing the dream, we join God in bringing his finished work to a world of decay and death, of despair and disease. We bring this finished work to free people from slavery and exploitation, spiritual bondage and hopelessness. The great dream of God is the dream for all the earth to flourish in every way. In our work in Christ's name, we herald that divine aspiration and intent. In the laughter of a child, the delicate dance of snow, flower petals at their peak and the wedding-day kiss of a giddy groom and bride, we see God's dream breaking in.

All these signal that the time is near—the end of one time and the beginning of another. Amid the gray and cold, amid want and questions, we see God's grace all around us—in the faces of the people of this world as well as in God's creation. In a foreshadowing of a world beyond belief, we have already tasted of the world we were created for.

The dream of God is coming. In some ways, it is already here, as the one who sits on the throne tells us today, "Behold! I am making all things new."

Acknowledgments

As one who has been perpetually consumed by the reality of Christ's coming, it has been a challenge for me to pay as much attention to this world as I do the next. I am grateful to many people over the years who have helped me to grow as a whole person—a father, husband, friend, leader and child of God. While this list undoubtedly is incomplete, I'd like to particularly thank my mentor and friend Barney Ford for pouring into my soul, helping me love my wife and children and preparing me for a deeper journey.

I am thankful to my friends on my personal board, Joe Moore, Ed Ollie, Ernie Katai, Rick Warren and Aaron Ammerman. You all have gifted me with joy and the understanding that life first and foremost revolves around my home and family. To my good friend Drew Wolford, you are a rare gift from God to me. Your passion for Christ and for his mission to the lost and least has reinfected and refueled me at this stage of life. Your passionate love for Colleen has inspired me in my marriage! I am also grateful to Dave Riddle and Jeff Hess—my "regular guys" for an irregular guy. Thanks for putting up with my love of fashion, obvious lack of power tools and understanding of sports, and all-around questionable "man card" credentials!

I am thankful for the music of Aradhna (www.aradhnamusic .com) which filled my ears with the echoes of the world to come while writing this entire book.

To my wife's family, "The Pennington Clan," there are too many of you to thank but I am grateful for free Sunday meals, rides on tractors/snowmobiles/4-wheelers, birthdays, Christmases, vacations and the occasional fight. I couldn't have asked for a more "normal" family. To my family, Mom, Bobby, Eric, Ragnar and Gary, I love you all and am fortunate to have a family that I can say honestly I love through and through!

Finally, and most importantly, I am thankful to my wife, Jodi, my daughters, Addison and Gabriella, and my son, Kiren. You all have inspired me to life in this world and the next. Your joy and love of life have marked my soul, and I will never be the same. I love you and the world you have made in our home.

Notes

[1]Arthur F. Glasser and Charles Edward van Engen, *Announcing the Kingdom: The Story of God's Mission in the Bible* (Grand Rapids: Baker Academic, 2003), p. 192.

[2]J. D. Douglas, *The New Bible Dictionary*, (Grand Rapids: Eerdmans, 1962), p. 1336.

[3]Bob Darden, *People Get Ready! A New History of Black Gospel Music* (New York: Continuum, 2004), p. 100.

[4]Andy Crouch, *Culture Making: Recovering Our Creative Calling* (Downers Grove, Ill.: InterVarsity Press, 2008), p. 169.

[5]I read this often-repeated quote on a plaque at the last stop of the Underground Railroad in Detroit.

[6]In the abolitionist community we use the word *commoditization* to refer to the assignment of value to that which ought not to be or traditionally is not a commodity, like people or relationships.

[7]*Dictionary.com Unabridged*, s.v. "indignation," accessed May 29, 2012, http://dictionary.reference.com/browse/indignation.

[8]Ralph Waldo Emerson and William H. Gilman, *The Journals and Miscellaneous Notebooks of Ralph Waldo Emerson* (Cambridge, Mass.: Belknap Press of Harvard University Press, 1960), p. 99.

[9]Kevin Jenkins, "For World Vision, Identity Is Strategy," address to World Vision Triennial Council, Kuala Lumpur, Malaysia, August 25, 2010.

[10]Ohio Trafficking in Persons Study Commission, Research and Analysis Sub-Committee, *Report on the Prevalence of Human Trafficking in Ohio*, www.ohioattorneygeneral.gov/getattachment/5880897e-09e5-4cd1-b051-4680ce560e6d/Report-on-the-Prevalence-of-Human-Trafficking-in-O.aspx.

[11]Quoted in Becky Benenate Teresa and Joseph Durepos, *No Greater Love* (Novato, Calif.: New World Library, 1997), p. 6.

About the Author

R. York Moore is the National Evangelist for InterVarsity Christian Fellowship/USA. He speaks widely on issues of global social injustice and is particularly passionate about the modern-day slave trade. As a modern-day abolitionist, R. York Moore has conducted "justice invitationals" throughout the United States in conjunction with many antislavery nongovernmental organizations. Working with political leaders, law enforcement, academicians, faith-based communities, business leaders and the medical community, Moore seeks to create sustainable solutions to the growing problem of modern-day slavery. Moore has led thousands to faith in Christ through the lens of justice, mobilizing them to follow Jesus into the world to make all things new for his kingdom. He and his wife live in Michigan, where he came to faith from atheism as a philosophy student at the University of Michigan.

R. YORK MOORE
National Evangelist
InterVarsity Christian Fellowship USA
PO Box 87753
Canton, MI 48187
www.tellthestory.net
Facebook/Twitter: yorkmoore